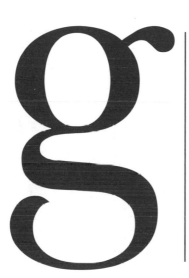

READING COMPREHENSION

Verbal Strategy Guide

This in-depth guide takes the mystery out of complex reading passages by providing a toolkit of sketching techniques that aim to build comprehension, speed, and accuracy. Learn to identify the underlying structure of reading passages and develop methods to tackle the toughest comprehension questions.

Reading Comprehension GMAT Strategy Guide, Fourth Edition

10-digit International Standard Book Number: 0-9824238-5-3
13-digit International Standard Book Number: 978-0-9824238-5-1

8 GUIDE INSTRUCTIONAL SERIES

Math GMAT Strategy Guides

Number Properties (ISBN: 978-0-9824238-4-4)

Fractions, Decimals, & Percents (ISBN: 978-0-9824238-2-0)

Equations, Inequalities, & VICs (ISBN: 978-0-9824238-1-3)

Word Translations (ISBN: 978-0-9824238-7-5)

Geometry (ISBN: 978-0-9824238-3-7)

Verbal GMAT Strategy Guides

Critical Reasoning (ISBN: 978-0-9824238-0-6)

Reading Comprehension (ISBN: 978-0-9824238-5-1)

Sentence Correction (ISBN: 978-0-9824238-6-8)

ManhattanGMAT
the new standard

July 1st, 2010

Dear Student,

Thank you for picking up one of the Manhattan GMAT Strategy Guides—we hope that this book makes it easier for you to read, understand, and solve Reading Comprehension passages and questions on the GMAT.

As with most accomplishments, there were many people involved in the various iterations of the book that you're holding. First and foremost is Zeke Vanderhoek, the founder of Manhattan GMAT. Zeke was a lone tutor in New York when he started the Company in 2000. Now, nine years later, MGMAT has Instructors and offices nationwide, and the Company contributes to the studies and successes of thousands of students each year.

Our 4th Edition Strategy Guides are based on the continuing experiences of our Instructors and our students. We owe much of these latest editions to the insight provided by our students. On the Company side, we are indebted to many of our Instructors, including but not limited to Josh Braslow, Dan Gonzalez, Mike Kim, Stacey Koprince, Ben Ku, Jadran Lee, David Mahler, Ron Purewal, Tate Shafer, Emily Sledge, and of course Chris Ryan, the Company's Lead Instructor and Director of Curriculum Development.

At Manhattan GMAT, we continually aspire to provide the best Instructors and resources possible. We hope that you'll find our dedication manifest in this book. If you have any comments or questions, please e-mail me at andrew.yang@manhattangmat.com. I'll be sure that your comments reach Chris and the rest of the team—and I'll read them too.

Best of luck in preparing for the GMAT!

Sincerely,

Andrew Yang
President
Manhattan GMAT

HOW TO ACCESS YOUR ONLINE RESOURCES

If you...

▶ **are a registered Manhattan GMAT student**

and have received this book as part of your course materials, you have AUTOMATIC access to ALL of our online resources. This includes all practice exams, question banks, and online updates to this book. To access these resources, follow the instructions in the Welcome Guide provided to you at the start of your program. Do NOT follow the instructions below.

▶ **purchased this book from the Manhattan GMAT Online store or at one of our Centers**

1. Go to: http://www.manhattangmat.com/practicecenter.cfm

2. Log in using the username and password used when your account was set up.

▶ **purchased this book at a retail location**

1. Create an account with Manhattan GMAT at the website: https://www.manhattangmat.com/createaccount.cfm

2. Go to: http://www.manhattangmat.com/access.cfm

3. Follow the instructions on the screen.

Your one year of online access begins on the day that you register your book at the above URL.

You only need to register your product ONCE at the above URL. To use your online resources any time AFTER you have completed the registration process, login to the following URL: http://www.manhattangmat.com/practicecenter.cfm

Please note that online access is non-transferable. This means that only NEW and UNREGISTERED copies of the book will grant you online access. Previously used books will not provide any online resources.

▶ **purchased an e-book version of this book**

1. Create an account with Manhattan GMAT at the website: https://www.manhattangmat.com/createaccount.cfm

2. Email a copy of your purchase receipt to books@manhattangmat.com to activate your resources. Please be sure to use the same email address to create an account that you used to purchase the e-book.

For any technical issues, email books@manhattangmat.com or call 800-576-4628.

Please refer to the following page for a description of the online resources that come with this book.

YOUR ONLINE RESOURCES

Your purchase includes ONLINE ACCESS to the following:

⊙ 6 Computer Adaptive Online Practice Exams

The 6 full-length computer adaptive practice exams included with the purchase of this book are delivered online using Manhattan GMAT's proprietary computer-adaptive test engine. The exams adapt to your ability level by drawing from a bank of more than 1,200 unique questions of varying difficulty levels written by Manhattan GMAT's expert instructors, all of whom have scored in the 99th percentile on the Official GMAT. At the end of each exam you will receive a score, an analysis of your results, and the opportunity to review detailed explanations for each question. You may choose to take the exams timed or untimed.

The content presented in this book is updated periodically to ensure that it reflects the GMAT's most current trends and is as accurate as possible. You may view any known errors or minor changes upon registering for online access.

Important Note: The 6 computer adaptive online exams included with the purchase of this book are the SAME exams that you receive upon purchasing ANY book in Manhattan GMAT's 8 Book Strategy Series.

⊙ *Reading Comprehension* Online Question Bank

The Bonus Online Question Bank for *Reading Comprehension* consists of 25 extra practice questions (with detailed explanations) that test the variety of concepts and skills covered in this book. These questions provide you with extra practice beyond the problem sets contained in this book. You may use our online timer to practice your pacing by setting time limits for each question in the bank.

⊙ Online Updates to the Contents in this Book

The content presented in this book is updated periodically to ensure that it reflects the GMAT's most current trends. You may view all updates, including any known errors or changes, upon registering for online access.

TABLE OF CONTENTS

g

Chapter 1
—*of*—
READING COMPREHENSION

INTRODUCTION TO PRINCIPLES

In This Chapter . . .

LOGISTICS OF READING COMPREHENSION

You are probably already familiar with Reading Comprehension from other standardized tests. You are given a passage to read, and you are asked questions about the substance and structure of the passage.

On the GMAT, you can expect to see **four** Reading Comprehension passages. Each passage will typically be accompanied by three to four questions, for a total of 12 to 14 Reading Comprehension questions. You should be aware of several logistical features of GMAT Reading Comprehension passages.

Passages are either long or short. GMAT Reading Comprehension passages come in two basic forms: LONG and SHORT. Long passages, which generally consist of over 300 words in three to five paragraphs, take up more than 50 lines on the computer screen (or over 35 lines in *The Official Guide for GMAT Review, 12th Edition* and *The Official Guide for GMAT Verbal Review, 2nd Edition*). Examples of long passages on the GMAT appear on pages 362, 366, and 382 of *The Official Guide for GMAT Review, 12th Edition*.

Short passages, which generally consist of 200–250 words in two or three paragraphs, take up fewer than 50 lines on the computer screen in length (or under 35 lines in *The Official Guide for GMAT Review, 12th Edition* and *The Official Guide for GMAT Verbal Review, 2nd Edition*). Examples of short passages on the GMAT appear on pages 358, 360, and 364 of *The Official Guide for GMAT Review, 12th Edition*.

In the past few years, short passages have been more common on the GMAT than long passages. Of the four passages that you see on the GMAT, three of them are likely to be short and one of them long. However, you might get two short and two long. Moreover, there is no set order in the appearance of short and long passages. Finally, the paragraphs themselves have been getting longer. You might see a long passage with only two paragraphs, or a short passage made up of only one paragraph.

Questions appear one at a time. The questions are presented one at a time on the right side of the computer screen. The complete reading passage remains on the left side of the screen while you answer questions on that passage. You will only be able to see the first question before reading the passage.

The number of questions per passage is NOT stated. The GMAT does not indicate how many questions are associated with a particular passage (i.e., the GMAT does not say that "Questions 6–9 refer to the following passage."). However, the length of the passage and the number of questions are strongly correlated. Generally, each short passage has three questions associated with it, and each long passage has four questions associated with it.

Line numbers are not listed. Though the Official Guide and older GMAT tests list line numbers down the side of the paragraphs, the GMAT itself does not now number the lines in each passage. When necessary, the GMAT will use yellow highlighting in the passage to indicate the location of a particular term, phrase or section.

> In order to determine your reading approach, first identify whether a passage is long or short.

Challenges of Reading Comprehension

The GMAT makes Reading Comprehension difficult in several ways.

The content is demanding. Passages focus on specific and often unfamiliar topics in physical science (physics, astronomy, geology, chemistry), biological science (biology, ecology), social science, history, and business. No specialized knowledge beyond high school is assumed, but the passages are written for an educated post-college audience. In fact, at least some of the passages seem to be adapted from journals published in particular fields for educated laypeople. You might be neither knowledgeable nor enthusiastic about these fields. Moreover, even business topics—which are probably inherently interesting to you, since you are planning to go to business school—are made tough by complex writing.

You have to read on screen. You cannot print the passage out and mark it up. Instead, you have to scroll a window up and down to see all of a long passage. Furthermore, reading on a computer screen is difficult on the eyes.

> Reading Comprehension passages do nor require specialized knowledge. Do not let jargon or complex sentences intimidate you.

You cannot preview all the questions. You cannot look over all the questions, glean ideas about what they are asking you, and <u>then</u> read the passage. Nor can you go back after answering a few more questions and change your response to the first question (now that you finally understand the passage). Rather, you have to grasp the content of the passage relatively well after your first read, having previewed only the first question.

You have to read quickly. You should only take at most four minutes to read a passage and understand it (2½ to 3 minutes for a short passage, 3½ to 4 minutes for a long passage). You may find Reading Comprehension frustrating for precisely this reason. If you had enough time, you could master almost any passage and answer almost any question correctly. But you do not have that luxury.

You have to stay with it. Reading Comprehension is the one question type that regularly asks three to four questions around one block of content. With every other GMAT question type, if you get completely stuck on the content of a particular question, you can always take a guess and move on to another question about something completely different without incurring too drastic a penalty. But you cannot afford to give up entirely on a Reading Comprehension passage, which can represent almost a tenth of the Verbal questions you face. So you must "tough it out" and wring a decent level of understanding out of every passage, no matter what.

Two Extremes and a Balanced Approach

One response to the challenges of Reading Comprehension is to become a **Hunter**. Hunters avoid the first read-through altogether, reasoning that most questions require some kind of detailed look-up anyway—so why not just skip the initial reading and go right to the questions? As their name implies, Hunters simply go "hunting" for the answer in a passage they have never read.

This strategy seems to save time up front, but you have to spend a lot more time per question. More importantly, the approach leads to many wrong answers. Without a good general understanding of the passage, Hunters can fall prey to trap answers.

At the other extreme, some GMAT test-takers become **Scholars.** Scholars do a very careful first read-through, paying attention to details. "After all," Scholars worry, "I could be asked about any aspect of the passage—and if I skim over anything, how can I be sure that that one clause was not important, even critical, to my overall understanding?"

One obvious problem with this method is that it takes far too much time. More important-ly, if you read <u>too</u> slowly and pay <u>too</u> much attention to all the details, you can easily lose sight of the big picture: the gist and structure of the whole passage. And the big picture is what you absolutely need to take away from the first read.

The middle ground between Hunters and Scholars is occupied by **Big Picture Readers**, who take a balanced approach. Before trying to answer the questions, they read the passage with an eye toward structure. At the beginning of the passage, Big Picture Readers go slow-ly, ensuring a solid grasp of the basics. But they go quickly at the end, keeping minor details at arm's length. They read ACTIVELY but EFFICIENTLY.

The goal of Big Picture Reading is to avoid finishing a passage and feeling that you just wasted your time—either because you got lost in the weeds, or because you skimmed over the passage at too removed a level to grasp any content.

How do you become a Big Picture Reader on the GMAT? Here are **Seven Principles of Active, Efficient Reading** to guide you.

Principle #1: Engage with the Passage

The first principle has to do with your <u>emotional attitude</u> toward the passage. The maxim *Engage with the Passage* is not as warm and fuzzy as it seems. It is based on a simple truth about your brain: you simply cannot learn something that you actively loathe or viscerally reject. So getting over your dread of the passage is not just a feel-good exercise. It is a pre-requisite. You do not have to fall madly in love with medieval Flemish poetry or the chem-istry of zinc, but you do have to stop keeping the topic at an emotional arm's length.

One quick and effective method is to **pretend that you really like this stuff**. Say to your-self, "This is great! I get to spend the next eight minutes thinking about *sea urchins*!" Who knows—you might actually like them, learn something along the way, and do well on the questions (the most important thing).

Another way to help yourself get into the passage psychologically is to **identify good guys and bad guys**. If the sea urchins are threatened by environmental damage, get a little angry on their behalf. If you engage your emotions, you will both enjoy the passage more and recall it better than otherwise.

If you cannot stomach these steps, **simply acknowledge that you do not find the passage thrilling.** Allow yourself a moment of disappointment. Then hunker down and get back into it. Whatever you do, do not let yourself be pushed around by the passage. Love it or hate it, you have to own it.

The next six principles have to do with your <u>cognitive processes</u>: what you do with your brain as you do a Big Picture Read. To illustrate these processes, we will construct an analo-gy. Imagine, if you will, that your brain is a <u>company's headquarters</u>.

Evaluate your approach to Reading Comprehension passages. Are you reading as efficiently and as effec tively as you could?

*Manhattan*GMAT*Prep

Recruiting for Your Working Memory, Inc.

More precisely, a <u>part</u> of your brain is like a company's headquarters: your **working memory**, where you store active thoughts. Your attention lives here. When you are thinking about sea urchins, your ideas about sea urchins live in your working memory. Only a few items fit at a time. Your working memory is the most valuable real estate in your brain.

Your job is to be the recruiter for the headquarters in your brain. A recruiter has two tasks: (1) to let <u>in</u> all the talented, important people AND (2) to keep <u>out</u> all the people who will not contribute.

As you read the passage, you have to act like a selective recruiter. You have to let the important parts into your working memory, but you also have to skim over the unimportant parts, so that you do not distract yourself with every last detail.

The next six principles explain how to be a good recruiter for your brain.

> Concentrate on the simple story within every GMAT passage. Armed with this simple story, you can answer general questions—and you know where to look for specific questions.

Principle #2: Look for the Simple Story

Every GMAT passage has a **simple story—the gist or core meaning of the passage**. You must find this simple story on the first read-through.

How do you identify this simple story? Here are three different methods. Also, for now, do not worry about whether, or how, you write down the simple story as you read a passage. Just focus on finding that story.

1. Text It To Me. As you read, ask yourself this question: how would you retell all this stuff to an intelligent but bored teenager in just a couple of sentences? Can you give him or her just 5–10 words to describe a paragraph? You will find yourself cutting out the trivia.

Simplifying does not contradict the principle of being engaged with the content of the passage. You should be extremely interested in the passage, so you know what is important.

2. Make a Table of Contents. Alternatively, you can create a short table of contents. Use five words or fewer for the headline of each paragraph. As written, these headlines may not sound exactly like a story, but they outline the same narrative.

3. Look for Content and Judgment. The parts of a simple story can generally be classified as Content or Judgment, as follows:

> <u>Content</u>: **the scientific or historical subject matter of the passage.**
>   (a) Causes (effects, evidence, logical results)
>   (b) Processes (steps, means, ends)
>   (c) Categories (examples, generalities)
>
> <u>Judgment</u>: **what the author and any other people believe about the Content.**
>   (a) Theories and Hypotheses
>   (b) Evaluations and Opinions
>   (c) Comparisons and Contrasts
>   (d) Advantages and Disadvantages

*Manhattan*GMAT*Prep
the new standard

Reminder: Don't Forget the Twist. Even as you look for the simple story, realize that on the GMAT, there will often be some important <u>qualification</u> or <u>contrast</u>—a **key twist** or two in the road. After all, such twists help the GMAT ask difficult questions. Be ready to incorporate a key twist or even two in your simple story.

For example, a passage might be about the worldwide decline in the population of frogs. In describing various theories, the passage might emphasize a distinction between the pessimistic theories shared by most scientists and the optimistic theory of one Scientist X, who believes that the decline is taking place within a natural oscillation.

The simple story might go like this:

> The number of frogs in the world is falling fast. There are a few possible explanations, including pollution, climate change, and loss of habitat. Most scientists think this decline is a serious problem caused by human activity, but Scientist X thinks it's part of a natural cycle and the frogs will come back soon on their own.

Here, the contrast is between what most scientists believe about the frog decline and what Scientist X believes.

Principle #3: Link to What You Already Know

When you read words on a page, they typically activate pre-existing knowledge in your head. This is a crucial part of comprehending what you are reading. Every word that you know in the English language is naturally tied to a web of memories and ideas. In fact, if a word does NOT activate ideas when you read it, it might as well be *zzyrglbzrch*!

Normally, your brain wakes up these ideas and memories as a natural part of reading. However, under stress, your eyes can pass over words and even recognize them, but no ideas come to life in your brain. You are too distracted and overwhelmed, and the words on the page remain "just words."

In this case, try **concretizing**. That is, **actively *imagine* what the words are referring to**. Re-explain the original text to yourself. Visualize what it represents. Indulge in simplifications, even stereotypes. Make up examples and use any other mental handles that you can.

Of course, there is a danger in actively concretizing part of a GMAT passage—you might introduce outside ideas. However, that danger is small in comparison to the worse problem of *not understanding at all* what you are reading, especially at the start of a passage.

Consider the following sentence, which could be the opening of a passage:

> Most exobiologists—scientists who search for life on other planets or moons—agree that carbon probably provides the backbone of any extraterrestrial biological molecules, just as it does of terrestrial ones, since carbon is unique among the elements in its ability to form long, stable chains of atoms.

Ideally, you can read this sentence and grasp it without any problems. But recognize that under pressure, you might need some help understanding the sentence.

You can think of the simple story in a few different ways. Regardless of your specific approach, remember the KISS principle: Keep It Simple, Stupid!

*Manhattan*GMAT*Prep
the new standard

In your mind, you might concretize this sentence in the following manner:

Words	Concretized Ideas
…exobiologists–scientists…	smart folks in white coats
…who search for life on other planets or moons…	who peer through telescopes looking for little green men
…carbon probably provides the backbone of extraterrestrial biological molecules…	carbon: charcoal, key element in living things backbone: like a spine to a little molecule
…its ability to form long, stable chains of atoms.	carbon can make long, stable chains like bones in a backbone or links in a physical chain

As you concretize, you may think of ideas not explicitly mentioned in the passage. That is normal. Just remember that those ideas were not actually mentioned in the passage.

You should NOT write this concretization down (except as an exercise during your preparation). The process should happen quickly in your head. Moreover, as you read further into the passage, the need to concretize should diminish. In fact, if you do too much concretizing along the way, you might introduce too many outside ideas and lose track of what is actually written in the passage. However, concretizing can help you make sense of a difficult passage, so you should practice this technique.

Principle #4: Unpack the Beginning

You must understand the first few sentences of every passage, because they supply critical context for the entire text. If you do not grasp these sentences at first, you have two choices. Either you can take more time with them right away, or you can read a little further and gather more context. In the latter case, you MUST go back and re-acquire those initial sentences later.

All too often, GMAT students satisfy themselves with an "impressionistic" sense of the beginning of a passage. However, **forming an impression is not comprehending the passage**. Given the importance of the initial sentences, you should make sure you grasp 100% of the beginning of any passage (even if you only grasp 40% of the end). That is far better than comprehending 70% of the text throughout.

Complicating matters, the GMAT often opens passages with long, opaque sentences. How do you make sure you understand them, either now or later? The process of concretizing can help. You can also use the **unpacking** technique. Academic language is often dense with long noun phrases formed out of simple sentences. **To unpack an academic-style sentence, turn it into a few simple sentences** that express essentially the same meaning.

In general, you should NOT write this unpacking out (except as an exercise) or apply it throughout the passage. Like concretizing, unpacking is a powerful tool to smash open resistant language, especially at the start of the passage. Use this technique judiciously.

The steps to unpacking a complex sentence are as follows:

1. Grab a concrete noun first. Pick something that you can touch and that causes other things to happen. Do not necessarily pick something at the start of the sentence.

2. Turn actions back into verbs. In academic language, verbs are often made into noun or adjective phrases. Re-create the verbs. Also, feel free to start with *There is* or *There was.*

3. Put only ONE simple thought in a sentence. One subject, one verb.

4. Link each subsequent sentence to the previous one, using *this* or *these.* For instance, *This resulted in…* This process mimics speech, which is usually easy to understand.

5. Simplify or "quote off" details. If a jargon word is used in an important way, put quotes around it. Think to yourself "…*whatever that means…*" and keep going. If the term is necessary, you will figure it out from context later.

Consider this example opening of a passage:

> In a diachronic investigation of possible behavioral changes resulting from accidental exposure in early childhood to environmental lead dust, two sample groups were tracked over decades.

1. Grab a concrete noun first, especially a cause. A good candidate is *lead dust.* The first sentence could simply be this: *There was lead dust in various environments.*

2. Turn other parts of speech, such as action nouns and adjectives, back into verbs. For instance, *exposure* becomes *were exposed. Behavioral* becomes *behaved.*

3. Put only one thought in a sentence, such as *There was lead dust in various environments.*

4. Link each sentence to the previous with *this/these.* So the second sentence could read *Young children in <u>these</u> environments were exposed to this dust by accident.*

5. Simplify or "quote off" details or jargon. For instance, the term *"diachronic"* needs a pair of quotes, so that you do not focus on it. You might even think of it just as "*d-*something."

The final list of a few simple sentences could come out this way:

> (1) There was lead dust in various environments.
> (2) Young children in these environments were exposed to this dust by accident.
> (3) This exposure may have changed how the children behaved.
> (4) This whole matter was investigated.
> (5) In this "diachronic" investigation, two sample groups were tracked over time.

This unpacked list is easier to dive into and understand than the original sentence—even though the list contains nearly twice as many words! Also note that the subject and verb of the original sentence do not appear until the end of the list. This phenomenon is very common. Often, it is easiest to understand the outer "frame" of the sentence <u>last</u>.

Concretizing and unpacking are powerful tools, but they take practice. Try them out in your everyday life. You will find dense text easier to understand.

Again, it is often not practical to employ such an elaborate process in real time on the GMAT. However, knowing how to break down a complex sentence into its component ideas can help you read more efficiently in general. In addition, you can use this technique if you are stuck on one of the early sentences, although it will require some effort.

Incidentally, the ten-dollar word *diachronic* means "happening over time" in certain technical settings. If you needed to know that word, you would be able to infer its meaning from context. For instance, the passage might contrast this decades-long *diachronic* investigation with a *synchronic* study of a cross-section of people all examined at one time. For the GMAT, you need to have an educated adult's working vocabulary, but you will not need advance knowledge of any specialized jargon.

Principle #5: Link to What You Have Just Read

As you read further, you must continue to ask yourself about the **meaning** and **purpose** of what you are reading. What does this sentence mean, in relation to everything else I have read? Why is this sentence here? What function does it serve in relation to the previous text?

In the unpacking technique, we saw the power of linking. Complicated ideas can be made digestible by breaking them into pieces and hooking them together. In writing, we do not always use *this* and *these*, but we often put references to old information at the beginning of sentences, even complex ones, to hook them to previous material. Likewise, we tend to save new information for the end of sentences.

What kinds of relationships can a sentence have to the previous text? In general, you should think about these possibilities:

> (1) Is the new sentence **expected or surprising**?
> (2) Does it **support or oppose** earlier material?
> (3) Does it **answer or ask** a question?

More specifically, the **Content/Judgment** framework that we encountered before can guide you. Do NOT use this framework as a checklist. Rather, simply be aware of the various possible relationships.

> <u>Content</u>: the scientific or historical subject matter of the passage.
> (a) Causes   (effects, evidence, logical results)
> (b) Processes   (steps, means, ends)
> (c) Categories (examples, generalities)

> <u>Judgment</u>: what the author and any other people believe about the Content.
> (a) Theories and Hypotheses
> (b) Evaluations and Opinions
> (c) Comparisons and Contrasts
> (d) Advantages and Disadvantages

Do not over-analyze as you read. You have been linking sentences together and making sense of them as a whole for many years—in fact, you are doing so now, as you read this chapter. We are just describing the process.

Principle #6: Pay Attention to Signals

To help link new material to previous text that you have read, you should be aware of various language signals.

First of all, **paragraph breaks** are important. They indicate something new. The sentences in the simple story often correspond to different paragraphs in the passage. If you take a "Table of Contents" approach to the simple story, your headlines correspond to the different paragraphs.

This does not mean that paragraphs cannot shift direction internally; they occasionally do. But paragraph breaks are not random. Each one marks a new beginning of some kind.

Second, **signal words** indicate relationships to previous text. Here are a number of such relationships, together with their common signals.

> Each paragraph generally represents a new chapter in the simple story, but paragraphs may include twists.

Relationship	Signal
Focus attention	As for; Regarding; In reference to
Add to previous point	Furthermore; Moreover; In addition; As well as; Also; Likewise; Too
Provide contrast	On one hand / On the other hand; While; Rather; Instead; In contrast; Alternatively
Provide conceding contrast (author unwillingly agrees)	Granted; It is true that; Certainly; Admittedly Despite; Although
Provide emphatic contrast (author asserts own position)	But; However; Even so; All the same; Still; That said Nevertheless; Nonetheless; Yet; Otherwise Despite [concession], [assertion]
Dismiss previous point	In any event; In any case
Point out similarity	Likewise; In the same way
Structure the discussion	First, Second, etc.; To begin with; Next; Finally; Again
Give example	For example; In particular; For instance
Generalize	In general; To a great extent; Broadly speaking
Sum up, perhaps with exception	In conclusion; In brief; Overall; Except for; Besides
Indicate logical result	Therefore; Thus; As a result; So; Accordingly; Hence
Indicate logical cause	Because; Since; As; Resulting from
Restate for clarity	In other words; That is; Namely; So to speak
Hedge or soften position	Apparently; At least; Can, Could, May, Might, Should; Possibly; Likely
Strengthen position	After all; Must, Have to; Always, Never, etc.
Introduce surprise	Actually; In fact; Indeed
Reveal author's attitude	Fortunately; Unfortunately; other adverbs; So-called

Principle #7: Pick Up the Pace

As you read the passage, go faster after the first paragraph. In your working memory, hold the growing jigsaw puzzle that is the big picture of the passage. As you read text later in the passage, ask whether what you are reading adds anything truly significant to that jigsaw puzzle. Toward the end, only dive into information that is clearly part of the big picture.

Do NOT get lost in details later on in the passage. Do NOT try to master every bit of content. You must read the whole passage—but keep later parts at arm's length.

Only pay close attention to the following elements later on in the passage:

> (1) **Beginnings of paragraphs**. The first or second sentence often functions as a topic sentence, indicating the content and/or purpose of the paragraph.
>
> (2) **Big surprises** or changes in direction.
>
> (3) **Big results**, answers or payoffs.

Everything else is just detail. Do not skip the later text entirely. You must pass your eyes over it and extract *some* meaning, so that if you are asked a specific question, you remember that you saw something about that particular point, and you know (sort of) where to look. Moreover, those big surprises and results can be buried in the middle of paragraphs. You must actually read the later paragraphs and make some sense of them.

Nevertheless, do not try to grasp the whole passage deeply the first time through. Your attention and your working memory are the most valuable assets you have on the GMAT in general and on Reading Comprehension in particular. Allocate these assets carefully.

Summary: The 7 Principles of Active, Efficient Reading

To become a Big Picture Reader of GMAT Reading Comprehension passages, follow these principles.

> **(1) Engage with the Passage**
>
> **(2) Look for the Simple Story**
>
> **(3) Link to What You Already Know**
>
> **(4) Unpack the Beginning**
>
> **(5) Link to What You Have Just Read**
>
> **(6) Pay Attention to Signals**
>
> **(7) Pick up the Pace**

Will you consciously go through each of these principles every time you read? Of course not. You need to practice them so that they become a natural part of your reading.

Practice on Non-GMAT Material

Reading Comprehension may seem difficult to improve, especially in a short period of time. However, you can accelerate your progress by applying these principles to what you read *outside* of the GMAT, as part of your daily life. Actively engage with the material, especially if you are not initially attracted to it. Look for the simple story. Link what you read to what you already know and to what you have just read. Unpack and/or concretize language if necessary. Pay attention to signals. And pick up the pace as you read, in order to avoid getting lost in details.

These principles work on a wide range of expository writing—a company's annual report, a book review in the newspaper, an article in your college alumni magazine. By applying these principles outside of a testing or test-prep environment, you will become much more comfortable with them.

Granted, some outside material is more GMAT-like than other material. You should read major journals and newspapers, such as *The Economist, The Wall Street Journal, The Atlantic Monthly,* and *The New York Times,* to become better informed about the world in general. However, these publications are somewhat *too* digestible. The paragraphs are too short, and neither the topics nor the writing itself is quite as boring as what you find on the GMAT.

In this regard, **university alumni magazines** are good sources of articles that resemble Reading Comprehension passages in style and substance. (No offense to our alma maters!) Also, if you are not naturally attracted to science topics, then you should consider reading a few articles in *Scientific American* or similar publications that popularize the latest advances in science and technology. In this way, you can gain familiarity with science writing aimed at an educated but non-specialized audience.

As you prepare for the GMAT, consider ratcheting up the complexity of your reading material, in order to practice making sense of dense text.

Problem Set

In problems #1–4, **concretize** each sentence. Focus on specific terms that you can visualize. Associate these terms with your knowledge and memories, and create a "mind's-eye" view of each sentence. Spend no more than 15–20 seconds per sentence. Then write down this concretization. (We do not suggest that you write down concretizations on the GMAT, but by writing them down now as part of this exercise, you can compare them to the sample answers and develop your ability to concretize.)

1. Computer models of potential terrestrial climate change over the next century must take into account certain assumptions about physical and chemical processes.

2. Company X has experienced a more rapid rate of growth than Company Y, because Company X has invested more resources in projects with a more rapid payout than has Company Y.

3. Given the complexity of the brain's perceptual and cognitive processes, it is not surprising that damage to even a small set of neurons can interfere with the execution of seemingly simple tasks.

4. The rise of Athenian democracy in ancient times can be considered a reaction to class conflict, most importantly between a native aristocracy and the inhabitants of nearby towns incorporated politically into the growing city-state.

In problems #5–8, **unpack** each complex sentence. That is, find a few simple sentences that convey the same information as the original sentence. Do the unpacking in your head first, then write down the unpacked sentences. (Do not write down unpacked sentences during the GMAT, but by writing them down now as part of this exercise, you can compare them to the sample answers and develop your ability to unpack.)

5. The simplistic classification of living things as plant, animal, or "other" has been drastically revised by biologists in reaction to the discovery of microorganisms that do not fit previous taxonomic schemes.

6. Despite assurances to the contrary by governments around the world, the development of space as an arena of warfare is nearly certain, as military success often depends on not ceding the "high ground," of which outer space might be considered the supreme example.

7. Since the success of modern digital surveillance does not obviate the need for intelligence gathered via old-fashioned human interaction, agencies charged with counter-terrorism responsibilities must devote significant effort to planting and/or cultivating "assets"—that is, spies—within terrorist organizations that threaten the country.

8. Students learning to fly fixed-wing aircraft are taught to use memory devices, such as the landing checklist GUMPS ("gas, undercarriage, mixture, propeller, switches"), that remain constant even when not every element of the device is relevant, as in the case of planes with non-retractable landing gear.

Read the following passage, and then complete the exercises on the next page.

Passage: Pro-Drop Languages

In many so-called "pro-drop" or "pronoun-drop" languages, verbs inflect for number and person. In other words, by adding a prefix or suffix or by changing in some other way, the verb itself indicates whether the subject is singular or plural, as well as whether the subject is first person (*I* or *we*), second person (*you*), or third person (*he*, *she*, *it*, or *they*). For example, in Portuguese, which is at least partially a pro-drop language, the verb *falo* means "I speak": the *–o* at the end of the word indicates first person, singular subject (as well as present tense). As a result, the subject pronoun *eu*, which means "I" in Portuguese, does not need to be used with *falo* except to emphasize who is doing the speaking.

It should be noted that not every language that drops its pronouns inflects its verbs. Neither Chinese nor Japanese verbs, for instance, change form at all to indicate number or person; however, personal pronouns are regularly omitted in both speech and writing, leaving the proper meaning to be inferred from contextual clues. Moreover, not every language that inflects its verbs drops subject pronouns in all non-emphatic contexts. Linguists argue about the pro-drop status of the Russian language, but there is no doubt that, although the Russian present-tense verb *govoryu* ("I speak") unambiguously indicates a first person, singular subject, it is common for Russian speakers to express "I speak" as *ya govoryu*, in which *ya* means "I," without indicating either emphasis or contrast.

Nevertheless, Russian speakers do frequently drop subject and object pronouns; one study of adult and child speech indicated a pro-drop rate of 40-80%. Moreover, personal pronouns must in fact be dropped in some Russian sentences in order to convey particular meanings. It seems safe to conjecture that languages whose verbs inflect unambiguously for person and number permit pronoun dropping, if only under certain circumstances, in order to accelerate communication without loss of meaning. After all, in these languages, both the subject pronoun and the verb inflection convey the same information, so there is no real need both to include the subject pronoun and to inflect the verb.

9.   Unpack the first two sentences of the first paragraph. That is, break them down into a series of simple linked sentences.

10. How does the second sentence of the first paragraph relate to the first sentence? What words indicate this relationship? Use the Content/Judgment framework, if it is helpful:

     Content: (a) Causes (effects; evidence; logical result)
                     (b) Processes (steps; means; end)
                     (c) Categories (example; generality)
     Judgment: (d) Theories/Hypotheses
                     (e) Evaluations/Opinions
                     (f) Comparisons/Contrasts
                     (g) Advantages/Disadvantages
                     (h) General Judgments (support/oppose; expected/surprising; answer/ask
                         questions)

11. How do the third and fourth sentences of the first paragraph relate to what came before? Use the Content/Judgment framework.

12. Analyze the second paragraph, using the Content/Judgment framework. What does this paragraph say, in brief? How does this paragraph relate to the first paragraph? Where are the big surprises and big results, if any?

13. Perform the same analysis on the third paragraph.

14. What is the simple story of this passage? Try one or more of these different styles:
     (a) Full Sentences
         • Summarize each paragraph in just a couple of sentences.
     (b) "Text It To Me"
         • Summarize each paragraph in 5–10 words or abbreviations.
         • Use symbols (such as = to equate two things).
         • Still try to express full thoughts.
     (c) Table of Contents
         • Give each paragraph a title or headline of no more than five words.
         • Do not try to express full thoughts.

Concretizations

These concretizations are specific examples. Your own concretizations will likely be different. Again, on the GMAT, you will *never* write down full concretizations such as these. Rather, you need to practice the process so that you can carry it out quickly in your head.

1.

Words	Concretized Ideas
Computer models of potential terrestrial climate change over the next century...	Big computers in some laboratory running programs about <u>potential terrestrial climate change</u> (how the Earth's weather might change) over the next 100 years...
...must take into account certain assumptions about physical and chemical processes.	These programs must know, or assume, how physics and chemistry works: how water heats up and evaporates, for instance.

2.

Words	Concretized Ideas
Company X has experienced a more rapid rate of growth than Company Y...	*Make up actual examples for Company X and Company Y. Make the examples extreme.* Vandelay Industries has grown very quickly, while Dunder Mifflin has hardly grown at all.
...because Company X has invested more resources in projects with a more rapid payout than has Company Y.	Vandelay has put more money into "quick hits." Maybe Vandelay has just hired some top salespeople who immediately generate revenue. Dunder Mifflin puts its money into longer-term projects. Maybe Dunder Mifflin is building laboratories for R&D.

3.

Words	Concretized Ideas
Given the complexity of the brain's perceptual and cognitive processes...	The brain is complex. It does complex things, like a computer in your skull. <u>perceptual</u>: how we see and hear <u>cognitive</u>: how we think and reason Given all that...
...it is not surprising that damage to even a small set of neurons...	...it is not surprising that just a little brain damage (say, caused by a small stroke), frying some wires in the computer...
...can interfere with the execution of seemingly simple tasks.	...can mess up how you do even "simple" things (say, speaking aloud or riding a bike). After all, your computer would probably stop working completely if you opened it up and ripped out "just a few" wires.

4.

Words	Concretized Ideas
The rise of Athenian democracy in ancient times...	Athenian democracy in ancient times: Socrates, Plato, Pericles, etc. voting in a public square. Marble statues and pillars everywhere.
...can be considered a reaction to class conflict...	You can think of all that as the result of <u>class conflict</u>: different economic and social groups struggling with each other. The workers versus the nobles.
...most importantly between a native aristocracy and the inhabitants of nearby towns incorporated politically into the growing city-state.	<u>Native aristocracy</u>: the rich & powerful people of Athens. They are struggling with the people from the provinces who are now under Athens' thumb. The map of "greater Athens" grows.

<u>Unpacking</u>

Like the concretizations, these unpacked sentences are simply examples of the process. Your versions will likely differ. Note that unpacking often involves some concretizing as well. Again, you should not write down unpacked sentences during the GMAT. This exercise is meant to develop your mental muscles, so you can take apart complex academic language.

5.   Living things can be classified as plant, animal, or "other."
This classification is simplistic.
In fact, it has been drastically revised by biologists.
Why? Because certain microorganisms (say, bacteria) have been discovered.
These microorganisms do not fit previous "taxonomic" schemes (that is, classifications).

6.   Space could be developed as an arena of warfare.
In fact, that's nearly certain to happen.
(Even though governments say otherwise.)
That's because to win wars, you often have to hold the "high ground."
And outer space may be the best "high ground" around.

7.   There is something called "modern digital surveillance" (say, spy bugs in cell phones).
This kind of surveillance has been successful.
But we still need people to gather "intelligence" by talking to other people.
So, the CIA etc. has to work hard to put "assets" (spies) inside Al Qaeda etc.

8.   There are people who learn to fly "fixed-wing aircraft."
These students learn memory devices.
An example of a memory device is GUMPS, which is a landing checklist.
These memory devices stay the same no matter what.
In fact, they stay the same even when part of the memory device does not apply.
An example is planes with "non-retractable" landing gear.

Passage: "Pro-Drop Languages"

9. The first two sentences could be unpacked in the following way:

> There are languages called "pronoun-drop" languages.
> In many of these languages, verbs "inflect" for number and person.
> That is, you change the verb itself somehow.
> This change shows who is doing the action (I, you, or someone else).
> The verb tells us whether that subject is singular or plural.
> The verb also tells us whether that subject is first, second, or third person.

10.   The second sentence restates and **explains** the first sentence. A clear clue is given by the first three words: *In other words*. The second sentence provides **specific examples** to help the reader understand a general assertion in the first sentence: *verbs inflect for number and person*. Also, the second sentence is **neutral in tone** and attitude.

11.   The third and fourth sentences provide an **even more specific example** of the phenomenon described in the first two sentences (*verbs inflect for number and person*). A clear clue is given at the start of the third sentence: *For example*. In the third sentence, we read about how the Portuguese verb *falo* is inflected. In the fourth sentence, we are told that the pronoun *eu* does not need to be used with *falo*. Again, the third and fourth sentences are **neutral in tone** and attitude.

12.   The second paragraph provides **qualification and contrast** to the first paragraph. The second paragraph also provides **specific examples** to support this contrast.

In brief, the second paragraph makes these points:

> • NOT every pro-drop language has verb inflections.
>> Example of Chinese & Japanese: pro-drop but not inflected.
> • NOT every inflected-verb language drops its pronouns, either!
>> Example of Russian: inflected but not pro-drop.

Logically, the categories of (A) "pro-drop" and (B) "inflected verbs" can be seen as overlapping circles on a Venn diagram. The assertion in the first paragraph is that these two circles overlap. In other words, *some A = B*. The second paragraph counters that these circles do not completely overlap, nor does one circle completely contain the other. That is, *NOT all A = B, and NOT all B = A.*

The "big surprises" and results are these two qualifications. You do not have to master the examples, although you should read them and make some sense of them. Moreover, at this stage, you might not grasp the nuances of the complicated Russian example. This is okay, as long as you understand the big picture of this paragraph.

13. In the first two sentences, the third paragraph provides a **contrast to the contrast** by continuing with the example of Russian, which turns out to be at least somewhat pro-drop.

Then the third paragraph proposes a **hypothesis** (inflected-verb languages are at least partially pro-drop) that follows from the Russian example. Finally, the paragraph offers a **rationale** for that hypothesis.

In brief, the third paragraph makes these points:
- Actually, Russian IS sometimes pro-drop.
- Hypothesis: Inflected-verb languages are at least partially pro-drop.
- Why? The inflection and the subject pronoun are redundant.

The switchback at the beginning might be considered a "big surprise." You need to grasp that the author is qualifying the example of the Russian language. Fortunately, you are given a clue in the very first word of the sentence, *Nevertheless*, which highlights a contrast to what came immediately prior. What follows *Nevertheless* is a position that the author wants to espouse.

The "big result" is the hypothesis in the third sentence. Note that this is the first time that the author goes beyond straight reporting and makes a claim: he or she states that *it is safe to conjecture* something.

14. The simple story of the passage can be expressed in at least three different styles.

Full Sentences
(1)   Many "pronoun-drop" languages have verbs that "inflect," or change.
- The inflected verb tells you something about the subject.
- So you can drop the subject pronoun.
- Portuguese is an example.

(2)   NOT every pro-drop language has verb inflections.
- Chinese & Japanese are examples.
Likewise, NOT every inflected-verb language is pro-drop!
- Russian is an example.

(3)   BUT, Russian is actually sort of pro-drop.
SO I think inflected-verb languages are all sort of pro-drop.
- Why? The inflected verb and the pronoun tell you the same thing.

Text It To Me
(1)   Pro-drop = inflect verbs. No subj.

(2)   Not all pro-drop = inflect. Not all inflect = pro-drop, either.

(3)   But actually, inflect = sort of pro-drop. Why repeat yrself.

Table of Contents
(1)   "Pronoun-Drop" Languages & Inflected Verbs

(2)   Exceptions Both Ways

(3)   Inflected Verbs = Pro-Drop Anyway

Chapter 2
of
READING COMPREHENSION

COMPONENTS
OF PASSAGES

In This Chapter . . .

- The Point
- Background, Support, and Implications
- Foreshadowing

COMPONENTS OF PASSAGES

Reading Comprehension passages cover a wide range of topics and are structured in many different ways. However, all passages have certain components. By understanding and looking for these components, you can more easily grasp the meaning and structure of the passage.

Any Reading Comprehension passage has four possible components:

(1) The Point
(2) Background
(3) Support
(4) Implications

We will consider each of these components in turn.

The Point

The Point is **the most important message of the passage**. In other words, the author has written the passage in order to convey the Point, even if nothing else gets through to the reader. The Point explains why the passage is interesting, at least in the author's opinion.

Every passage contains a Point. Perhaps surprisingly, the Point is often made explicit in a single sentence. In the "Pro-Drop Languages" passage from last chapter, the Point is the hypothesis put forward in the third paragraph:

> It seems safe to conjecture that **languages whose verbs inflect unambiguously for person and number permit pronoun dropping**, if only under certain circumstances, in order to accelerate communication without loss of meaning.

The author wants us to remember this Point. Of course, the author also wants us to understand how many pro drop languages work in general, how some pro-drop languages do not inflect their verbs, and so forth. But the most important message is this hypothesis, which is also the most important claim that the author puts forward.

How does the Point relate to the simple story of the passage, as discussed in Chapter 1? Very simply, **the Point is the crux of the simple story**. After all, the Point is the most important message that the author wants to convey. We can also relate the Point to the Content/Judgment framework. The Point contains the most important Judgment made by the author about the central Content of the passage.

Thus, a crucial task for you as reader is to **find the Point**! By the end of your first read-through, you should think about the simple story you have constructed. Use it to identify the Point.

Where is the Point in the passage? It can be almost anywhere. The way to find the Point is to ask "what is the most important message that the author is trying to convey in this passage? If he or she had to choose, what would be the one thing I should take away from reading this passage?"

The four components of a passage provide simple categories that allow you to identify a passage's structure and meaning more easily.

The Point may be any kind of important message, but across sample passages, we observe a few common varieties that sometimes overlap:

(a) **Resolution**: resolves an issue or a problem
(b) **Answer:** answers a question (similar to Resolution)
(c) **New Idea**: describes a surprising new idea, theory or research result
(d) **Reason**: explains an observation

During the GMAT, you will *not* have to classify the Point as one of the preceding types. Rather, this list is meant to help you identify and understand the Point as you read a variety of passages.

Notice that **the Point is related to a passage's purpose**. The point is what the author wants to *convey*. The purpose of a passage is generally to convey that Point. However, the purpose can often be described more broadly or abstractly as well. For instance, the purpose of the "Pro-Drop Languages" passage is to describe how languages may be categorized as pro-drop and as verb-inflecting, and to discuss the complex relationship between these two types of languages.

Also note that the Point may not make a lot of sense on its own. For instance, in order to understand and be convinced that *languages whose verbs inflect unambiguously for person and number permit pronoun dropping*, you need to understand the rest of the "Pro-Drop Languages" passage.

Occasionally, the Point is spread across two sentences, or it may be less than explicit. However, most passages have a clear Point within a single sentence.

If you have already started to study Critical Reasoning, you might suspect that the Point of a Reading Comprehension passage is similar to the conclusion of a Critical Reasoning argument. You are right! **The Point of a passage is in fact analogous to the conclusion of an argument**.

Note that passages do not always make impassioned arguments or take strong positions, so the Point of a passage might be less of a "claim" than the conclusion of an argument. Sometimes the Point of a passage is just the most interesting and general fact about the topic. The author may simply wish to inform the reader of this fact, rather than convince the reader of a debatable position.

Simply looking for the Point as you read will make you a more active reader. You will find that your comprehension of each passage will improve as a result.

Background, Support, and Implications

The other components all relate to the Point in some way.

1. **The Background is information you need to understand the Point.** The context and the basic facts about the topic are given in the Background. This component may be brief.

2. **The Support is evidence, assertions, and opinions FOR the Point.** The Support might

> A passage's Point is similar to an argument's conclusion. However, a Point is sometimes less of an impassioned claim and more of an interesting idea.

include concessions to the other side of the argument. This component is always present and often constitutes a substantial portion of the passage.

The Background and the Support may be intertwined. It is never important to determine whether a particular sentence is Background or Support. A sentence can provide background information and support the Point at the same time.

3. **The Implications are results from the Point**. In other words, the author now assumes that you are convinced of the Point and so begins to enumerate the consequences. Implications are not always present, but when they are, they tend to be important. The GMAT likes to ask questions about the Implications.

Although you do not have to separate Background and Support in every case, you should understand what you are reading in terms of the four components:

- Is this the main message? If so, this is the Point.
- Is this just background information? If so, this is Background.
- Is this supporting evidence for the main message? If so, this is Support.
- Is this an implication of the main message? If so, this is an Implication.

When you notice foreshadowing, use it to help you identify the Point.

Foreshadowing

In roughly 2/3 of the passages in the Official Guide, some part of the Background or the Support also functions as foreshadowing. **Foreshadowing sets up the Point.** It often does so by standing in contrast to the Point.

Foreshadowing		Point
Problem..................	leads to..........	Resolution
Question..................	leads to..........	Answer
Old Idea....................	leads to..........	New Idea
Observation..............	leads to..........	Reason or New Idea

An Old Idea might be a typical expectation or way of thinking (e.g., *Traditionally, lower returns on investments correlate with lower risk*). An Observation often expresses not only a fact but also an opinion about that fact (e.g., *The decision about where to store high-level nuclear waste for millennia has unfortunately not been resolved*). Note that in both of these examples, an adverb (*traditionally, unfortunately*) sets up a contrast that will be made explicit with the Point.

Note that just as you will never have to classify the Point on the GMAT, you will not have to classify the foreshadowing. This list is only meant to help you identify and understand the relationships between any foreshadowing and the Point.

Foreshadowing is not always present. Do not rely on foreshadowing to identify the Point. However, if foreshadowing is present, it can help you to find the Point more quickly and easily.

Problem Set

Answer the questions below by referring to the following passage.

Passage: Rock Flour

Although organic agriculture may seem to be the wave of the future, some experts believe that the next stage in agricultural development requires the widespread adoption of something very inorganic: fertilizer made from powdered rocks, also known as "rock flour." The biochemical processes of life depend not only on elements commonly associated with living organisms, such as oxygen, hydrogen, and carbon (the fundamental element of organic chemistry), but also on many other elements in the periodic table. Specifically, plants need the so-called "big six" nutrients: nitrogen, phosphorus, potassium, calcium, sulfur, and magnesium. In modern industrial agriculture, these nutrients are commonly supplied by traditional chemical fertilizers. However, these fertilizers omit trace elements, such as iron, molybdenum and manganese, that are components of essential plant enzymes and pigments. For instance, the green pigment chlorophyll, which turns sunlight into energy that plants can use, requires iron. As crops are harvested, the necessary trace elements are not replaced and become depleted in the soil. Eventually, crop yields diminish, despite the application or even over-application of traditional fertilizers. Rock flour, produced in abundance by quarry and mining operations, may be able to replenish trace elements cheaply and increase crop yields dramatically.

Not all rock flour would be suitable for use as fertilizer. Certain chemical elements, such as lead and cadmium, are poisonous to humans; thus, applying rock flour containing significant amounts of such elements to farmland would be inappropriate, even if the crops themselves do not accumulate the poisons, because human contact could result directly or indirectly (e.g., via soil runoff into water supplies). However, most rock flour produced by quarries seems safe for use. After all, glaciers have been creating natural rock flour for thousands of years as they advance and retreat, grinding up the ground underneath. Glacial runoff carries this rock flour into rivers, and downstream, the resulting alluvial deposits are extremely fertile. If the use of man-made rock flour is incorporated into agricultural practices, it may be possible to make open plains as rich as alluvial soils. Such increases in agricultural productivity will be necessary to feed an ever more crowded world.

1. What is the Point of this passage? Justify your choice. Categorize the Point: (a) Resolution, (b) Answer, (c) New Idea, or (d) Reason. (The Point may fall into more than one category.)

2. Identify the other components of the passage, if present: Background, Support, and Implications. Again, justify your assignments.

3. Identify any foreshadowing, if present. If there is foreshadowing, categorize it: (a) Problem, (b) Question, (d) Old Idea, or (d) Observation. (Like the Point, foreshadowing may fall into more than one category.)

4. What is the simple story of this passage?

1. The Point of this passage is contained in the first sentence of the first paragraph: *Some experts believe that the next stage in agricultural development requires the widespread adoption of something very inorganic: fertilizer made from powdered rocks, also known as "rock flour."* This is the most important message that the author intends to convey.

Two other candidates for the Point say nearly the same thing, as they extol the potential benefits of rock flour. In fact, these other sentences are perhaps even more emphatic than the Point itself, but they are slightly narrower in scope.

(a) Last sentence, first paragraph: *Rock flour... may be able to replenish trace elements cheaply and increase crop yields dramatically.* This sentence explains <u>how</u> rock flour may be able to help us achieve *the next stage in agricultural development.* Thus, this sentence is Support for the Point.

(b) Second to last sentence, second paragraph: *If the use of man-made rock flour is incorporated into agricultural practices, it may be possible to make open plains as rich as alluvial soils.* This sentence practically restates the Point in concrete terms. However, those concrete terms (*open plains, alluvial soils*) are more specific than the Point. Thus, this sentence should also be classified as Support for the Point.

Categorization of the Point:
The Point is a New Idea: a new type of fertilizer that may seem surprising initially. Alternatively, the Point can be considered the Resolution to a Problem (the depletion of trace elements essential for plant growth). As was mentioned in the text, it is not important for you to determine whether the Point is a New Idea or a Resolution; it could be both. These categories are only there to help you recognize and understand the Point.

2. The other parts of the passage can be labeled thus.

Background:	First paragraph	
	First clause, first sentence:	*Although organic agriculture... future,*
	Second sentence:	*The biochemical processes... periodic table.*
	Third sentence:	*Specifically,... magnesium.*
	Fourth sentence:	*In modern... traditional chemical fertilizers.*

These sentences give information, but they do not delineate the problem that must be solved.

Support:	First paragraph	
	Fifth sentence:	*However, these fertilizers omit... pigments.*
	all the way through to	
	Second paragraph	
	Second to last sentence:	*If the use... alluvial soils.*

This Support begins from the *However*, which introduces the problem. The rest of that paragraph explains the problem that rock flour solves.

Note that the Support includes the qualifications and concessions in the first half of the second paragraph.

Implications: <u>Second paragraph</u>
                 Last sentence: *Such increases... more crowded world.*

This sentence tells us the result of the Point. That is, if you accept the Point, then with the *resulting increases in agricultural productivity*, we may able to *feed the world!*

3. The first clause of the first sentence (*Although organic agriculture may seem to be the wave of the future*) is foreshadowing. This foreshadowing sets up the Point by telling us what may <u>seem</u> to be the solution (implying that something else IS the solution). Note that this foreshadowing is immediately followed by the Point itself. This juxtaposition is not unusual.

The category of foreshadowing is Old Idea (the old "new idea" of *organic agriculture*, as the author implies). Thus, we can now see that the Point is really New Idea: an idea that may solve a problem, of course, but we do not learn about that problem in the foreshadowing.

4. As we saw in the last chapter, the simple story of the passage can be expressed in at least three different styles.

<u>Full Sentences</u>
(1)   Some think the future of agriculture depends on rock flour (= powdered rock).
           • Plants require certain elements.
           • Normal fertilizers do not give you the <u>trace</u> elements such as iron.
           • Rock flour might fill the gap.
(2)   Some rock flour is bad, even poisonous.
        BUT most would be fine.
        Glaciers make natural rock flour which is good for the soil.
        If we use rock flour, maybe we can feed the world.

<u>Text It To Me</u>
(1)   Agricult. future = rock flour (= powder). Gives plants missing trace elems.
(2)   Some flour = bad. But glaciers make it & it's good. Might feed the world.

<u>Table of Contents</u>
(1)   Rock Flour as Future of Agriculture
(2)   Concerns; Reassuring Glaciers

Chapter 3
of
READING COMPREHENSION

SHORT
PASSAGES

In This Chapter . . .

- Short Passages: An Overview
- Don't Just Read, Do Something!
- The Headline List
- Common Notations
- Using Your Headline List
- Timing for Short Passages
- Common Structures of Short Passages
- Model Short Passage: **Insect Behavior**
- Model Headline List: **Insect Behavior**

SHORT PASSAGES: AN OVERVIEW

As noted in Chapter 1, short passages are fewer than 50 lines on the computer screen in length (or under 35 lines in the Official Guide). Short passages consist of 200-250 words in two or three short paragraphs, although a few passages consist of just one paragraph.

To approach short passages, recall the Seven Principles of Active, Efficient Reading:

> (1) Engage with the Passage
> (2) Look for the Simple Story
> (3) Link to What You Already Know
> (4) Unpack the Beginning
> (5) Link to What You Have Just Read
> (6) Pay Attention to Signals
> (7) Pick up the Pace

Imagine that you are taking the GMAT and up pops a new Reading Comprehension passage. How do you apply these reading principles? Let us imagine two scenarios:

> Positive Scenario: you are feeling good about your performance on the GMAT overall and on the Verbal section in particular. You are on pace or even ahead of pace. You are focused and energetic. Even better, the passage is about killer whales—and you happen to have majored in marine biology, a subject close to your heart.

> Negative Scenario: you are feeling anxious about your performance on the GMAT overall and on the Verbal section in particular. You are short on time. You are tired and scatterbrained. Making matters even worse, the passage is about killer whales— and you happen to hate biology. You even dislike the ocean.

In the Positive Scenario, it will be easy for you to apply the Seven Principles. You love the subject, you already know something about it, and you are in good shape on the exam. In this case, what you should do is **simply read the passage**. Enjoy it as you quickly digest it; simply be sure not to bring in outside knowledge. In the Positive Scenario, you can read the passage rapidly, easily, and effectively, and you can then move to answering the questions, a subject we will cover later in this book.

The Negative Scenario might happen to you during the GMAT. In fact, it is likely that you will be stressed at least some of the time during the exam. Moreover, even in the best of circumstances, you *might* find that one out of four passages falls on your "home turf" of topics. The other three will probably be unfamiliar territory. In addition, the GMAT makes otherwise interesting passages as boring and tedious as possible by using dry, clinical language and overloading the passages with details.

So how do you apply the Seven Principles in the Negative Scenario: that is, when the passage is unfriendly and you are stressed out?

Creating a Headline List for a short passage builds comprehension and promotes speed without getting you bogged down in the details.

Don't Just Read, Do Something!

The temptation will be simply to read the passage and then jump into the questions. The problem with this approach is that your grasp of the passage will be superficial. Moderately difficult questions will trick or stump you. You will have to reread the passage non-systematically. In fact, you might even answer every question without feeling that you *ever* understood this passage!

When the passage is unfriendly, you should NOT *just* read it!

There is a better way. We use three general methods to learn something new:

    (1) We read, as when we read a college textbook (or this guide).
    (2) We write, as when we take notes during a college lecture.
    (3) We listen, as during a lecture in a college course.

You can build your comprehension more quickly and effectively—*especially* when the passage is unfriendly—by using more than one learning method. Under normal circumstances you cannot have someone read the passage aloud to you. Nor can you read the passage aloud to yourself (although you might benefit from mouthing it or *quietly* mumbling to yourself). Thus, **you should make use of WRITING**, which activates a second learning process that facilitates comprehension.

Identifying <u>and writing down</u> key elements of the passage will force you to read ACTIVELY as opposed to passively. If you write in the right way, your comprehension of unfriendly or even neutral passages will improve dramatically. Indeed, you should develop a writing strategy for *every* passage during practice, because you need that strategy to be robust under all circumstances.

Of course, it is not possible to rewrite an entire passage in the time allocated for Reading Comprehension questions. But even writing and summarizing key elements will help you understand the structure and content of a passage while saving you time for questions.

Now, what you write during the GMAT must be different from other kinds of notes you have taken (e.g., during a college lecture). In college, you take notes in order to study from them later. In contrast, **you take notes during the GMAT in order to create comprehension right there and then.** This is a very different goal. In fact, you should take notes that, in theory, you could *crumple up and throw away* before answering any questions, if you were forced to. Why take notes, then? To force your mind to carry out the Seven Principles of Active, Effective Reading—*not* to study for some later test. So you must fundamentally change your approach to taking notes.

You should NOT plan to use your notes afterwards very much, because then you will be tempted to write too much down. If you write too much down, you will get lost in the details, and you will spend too much time. *Knowing* that you are spending too much time, you will become even more stressed. Thus, your level of comprehension will decrease. Eventually, you may abandon note-taking altogether. If you do so, you will not have an effective strategy for unfriendly passages. So, **imagine that you have limited ink**. Everything that you write down should pass a high bar of importance.

Read tough passages actively by taking efficient notes.

What kinds of notes should you take? **You should take notes that allow you to grasp the simple story of the passage**.

That does not mean that you should necessarily write down the simple story in full sentences. Generally, you should try to be more abbreviated. Use the "Text It To Me" style (a full thought in 5-10 words) or the "Table of Contents" style (a headline of five words or fewer). We call these notes of the simple story the HEADLINE LIST of the passage.

When you encounter a short passage, create a Headline List of the passage during your first reading.

A Headline List serves several purposes:

(1) It fosters an understanding of the content and purpose of the passage by using writing to enable active reading.

(2) It provides a general structure without getting you bogged down in details.

(3) It promotes a fast first reading of a passage that still gives you enough time to answer questions.

Do not worry about taking neat notes. Focus on the real goal: creating true comprehension quickly.

The Headline List

To create a Headline List, follow these steps:

1. A headline summarizes and conveys the main idea of a newspaper article. Likewise, **your Headline List should summarize or indicate the main idea of each paragraph.**

Most paragraphs have one topic sentence. Generally, the topic sentence is the first or second sentence, although it can also be a combination of the two.

Read the first sentence or two of the first paragraph. Identify the topic sentence and summarize it concisely on your scratch paper in the form of a headline. Use either the "Text It To Me" style or the "Table of Contents" style (a headline of 5 words or fewer). If you cannot identify a topic sentence, then your headline should summarize the main idea or purpose of the paragraph in your own words.

2. Read the rest of the paragraph with an eye for big hidden surprises or results.

As you read the rest of the paragraph, briefly summarize anything else that is very important or surprising in the paragraph. Often, this will consist of simply jotting down a word or two. You may in fact not add anything to the original topic sentence if the paragraph fits neatly within the scope of that sentence.

3. Follow the same process for subsequent paragraphs.

Each paragraph may introduce a whole new idea. Therefore, your approach to each subsequent paragraph should be the same as with the first paragraph. As you create your Headline List, make it coherent. The parts should relate to each other.

How much do you read before stopping to take notes? It depends. If the passage is really tough, slow down and go sentence by sentence. If the passage is easier and you think you are getting it, read more (even a whole paragraph) before taking notes on that chunk. Stopping to take notes can take you out of the "flow." At the same time, you should force yourself to stop periodically and consider adding to your Headline List.

4. Once you have finished the passage, identify the passage's Point.

After you have finished reading the passage and creating the Headline List, glance back over your notes and over the passage. Make sure you know what the Point of the passage is. If it is not in your Headline List already, be sure to add it. Then, label or mark the Point, so that you articulate it to yourself. This way, you are certain of the author's most important message. Now proceed to the first question.

Common Notations

To create your Headline List as quickly as possible, consider the following notations:

(1) Abbreviate long terms, particularly proper nouns.

(2) Use arrows (e.g. →) to indicate cause-effect relationships or changes over time.

(3) If a passage contains speakers, writers, points-of-view, arguments, etc., keep them organized by placing the person with the opinion before a given opinion with a colon. For example: **Historians: econ. interests → war.**

(4) If you write down examples, mark them with parentheses or "Ex." For example: **Insects = inflexible (sphex wasp).**

(5) Number each paragraph. Paragraph breaks are important to remember.

You will have your own note-taking style. For instance, if you are a visual thinker, you may draw pictures or use graphs to show relationships. Regardless of the notations you use, practice them and keep them CONSISTENT.

Using Your Headline List

How do you use your Headline List to answer questions about the passage? As mentioned above, you should avoid having to use the Headline List at all! You should already understand the simple story of the passage. Thus, you should be able to answer all GENERAL questions without referring either to your notes or to the passage. General questions pertain to the passage's main idea, its purpose, its structure, or its tone. The first question, which is visible along with the passage initially, is often a General question.

As for SPECIFIC questions, you will have to return to the passage to find particular details. In many cases, you will be able to find the relevant details on your own. But you can also use your Headline List as a search tool, so that you can locate the paragraph that contains the detail. You may have even jotted the detail down, if it struck you as important at the time.

ManhattanGMAT Prep
the new standard

If a paragraph in a short passage does not have one topic sentence, create headlines for the main points of that paragraph instead.

Timing for Short Passages

Overall, you have approximately one minute and forty-five seconds per question on the GMAT Verbal section. However, you should plan on taking a little more time on Reading Comprehension questions.

To determine how much time to spend on a passage, use this rule: **you have two minutes per Reading Comprehension question, total.** The total number of minutes includes time for reading the passage, creating a Headline List, and answering all the questions. Typically, each short passage has three questions associated with it. Thus, you have roughly **six minutes** to read and sketch the short passage and then answer the associated questions.

Out of this six-minute period, you should spend approximately 2.5–3 minutes reading the passage and generating your Headline List. Then you should spend between 60 and 75 seconds actually answering each question. The first question will often be a General question. You should try to answer General questions within 60 seconds. Specific questions will be more time-consuming, since they demand that you review the text of the passage. You should allocate up to 75 seconds for any Specific question.

You can best learn to create Headline Lists with repeated practice. Study the model on the next page, then do the In-Action exercises. Later, for more practice, create Headline Lists for Official Guide passages.

Spend approximately 6 minutes reading, creating a Headline List, and answering all the questions for a given short passage.

Common Structures of Short Passages

Short passages often display one of the following three structures. The first two are the most common. By recognizing these structures, you can decipher difficult passages more rapidly.

Point First	Point Last	(Point in Middle)
POINT *E.g., **X is true***	Background *E.g., Phenomenon Q happens*	Background *E.g., Phenomenon Q happens*
Support *Here's why*	Support *There is theory X There is theory Y Pros & cons*	**POINT** ***Theory X explains Q***
(Optional Implications) *Here's what could result*	**POINT** ***Theory X is better***	Support *Here's why*
		(Optional Implic.)

When the Point comes first, it might be in sentence #2 (sentence #1 would then be fore-shadowing). Likewise, "Point Last" means "Point in the last 2 sentences." When the Point comes later in the passage, there is frequently foreshadowing earlier. Of course, the GMAT is not limited to these structures. In some short passages, the Point is split up; the pieces are located in more than one place in the passage.

Model Short Passage: *Insect Behavior*

Insect behavior generally appears to be explicable in terms of unconscious stimulus–response mechanisms; when scrutinized, it often reveals a stereotyped, inflexible quality. A classic example is the behavior of the female sphex wasp. In a typical case, the mother leaves her egg sealed in a burrow alongside a paralyzed grasshopper, which her larva can eat when it hatches. Before she deposits the grasshopper in the burrow, she leaves it at the entrance and goes inside to inspect the burrow. If the inspection reveals no problems, she drags the grasshopper inside by its antennae. Scientific experiments have uncovered an inability on the wasp's part to change its behavior when experiencing disruptions of this routine.

Charles Darwin discovered that if the grasshopper's antennae are removed the wasp will not drag it into the burrow, even though the legs or ovipositor could serve the same function as the antennae. Later Jean-Henri Fabre found more evidence of the wasp's dependence on predetermined routine. While a wasp was performing her inspection of a burrow, he moved the grasshopper a few centimeters away from the burrow's mouth. The wasp brought the grasshopper back to the edge of the burrow, then began a whole new inspection. When Fabre took this opportunity to move the food again, the wasp repeated her routine. Fabre performed his disruptive maneuver forty times, and the wasp's response never changed.

Remember to read as if you enjoy learning about insect behavior!

Model Headline List for *Insect Behavior*

1) Insect behav. = unconsc. stim/resp. = inflexible   ← Point
   -- Ex: wasp can't change

2) D: wasp won't drag g. w/o anten.
   F: similar evid

The Headline List summarizes the topic sentence of the first paragraph, and the example is briefly listed. The second paragraph does not have a single topic sentence (two separate experiments are described), so the Headline List simply bullet-points the two experiments. Note that single letters (*g*) can stand for whole words. Remember that you are not taking notes that you need to study from later!

In this example, the Point of the passage is the first sentence of the first paragraph. The rest of the passage is Support for the Point. The structure of the passage is thus Point First.

Problem Set

1. Read the following passage and create a Headline List within 2.5–3 minutes. After answering the questions below the passage, compare your Headline List to the sample in the answer key. How well did your Headline List succeed in pushing you to read actively? How well did it capture the simple story of the passage without getting bloated with details?

Passage: Arousal and Attraction

In 1974, psychologists Donald Dutton and Arthur Aron conducted a study to determine the effects of physiological arousal on perceived attractiveness. Capilano Canyon in British Columbia is spanned by two bridges: one a swaying wire-suspension footbridge hundreds of feet in the air, and the other a solid wood bridge with high handrails, situated only a few feet above a shallow river. Male subjects crossing the bridges were met by an attractive female interviewer, who asked them to respond to a questionnaire that secretly measured sexual arousal. Subjects crossing the wire-suspension bridge responded with significantly more sexual imagery than the subjects crossing the solid bridge. Moreover, the interviewer gave each respondent her phone number and invited him to call later in order to discuss the study further. Half of the respondents crossing the wire-suspension bridge called later, versus 13% of those crossing the solid bridge. These results were not replicated with a male interviewer.

Dutton and Aron explained their results in terms of a misattribution. In their view, the males crossing the wobbly footbridge experienced physical reactions of fear, such as increased heart rate. Upon encountering a potential mate, the males reinterpreted these physiological effects as evidence of attraction to the female. In this view, strong emotions with ambiguous or suppressed causes would be reinterpreted, in the presence of a potential partner, as sexual attraction. This view seems to have persisted until Foster and others found in 1998 that an unattractive interviewer is actually perceived as less attractive by those crossing the wire-suspension bridge than by those crossing the solid bridge. As a result, the true effect is probably one of polarization: physiological arousal is reinterpreted as sexual attraction in the presence of an attractive partner, but as repulsion in the presence of an unattractive partner.

2. What is the Point of this passage? Justify your choice.

3. Identify the other components of the passage, if present: Background, Support, and Implications. Again, justify your assignments.

4. What is the structure of this passage? In other words, where is the Point positioned, and why?

5. Read the following passage and create a Headline List in 2.5–3 minutes. After answering the questions below the passage, compare your Headline List to the sample in the answer key and provide critiques.

Passage: Animal Treatment

Over the course of the eighteenth and early nineteenth centuries, educated Britons came to embrace the notion that animals must be treated humanely. By 1822 Parliament had outlawed certain forms of cruelty to domestic animals, and by 1824 reformers had founded the Society for the Prevention of Cruelty to Animals.

This growth in humane feelings was part of a broader embrace of compassionate ideals. One of the great movements of the age was abolitionism, but there were many other such causes. In 1785 a Society for the Relief of Persons Imprisoned for Small Sums persuaded Parliament to limit that archaic punishment. There was also a Society for Bettering the Condition of the Poor, founded in 1796. A Philanthropic Society founded in 1788 provided for abandoned children. Charity schools, schools of midwifery, and hospitals for the poor were being endowed. This growth in concern for human suffering encouraged reformers to reject animal suffering as well.

Industrialization and the growth of towns also contributed to the increase in concern for animals. The people who protested against cruelty to animals tended to be city folk who thought of animals as pets rather than as livestock. It was not just animals, but all of nature, that came to be seen differently as Britain industrialized. Nature was no longer a menacing force that had to be subdued, for society's "victory" over wilderness was conspicuous everywhere. A new sensibility, which viewed animals and wild nature as things to be respected and preserved, replaced the old adversarial relationship. Indeed, animals were to some extent romanticized as emblems of a bucolic, pre-industrial age.

6. What is the Point of this passage? Justify your choice.

7. Identify the other components of the passage, if present: Background, Support, and Implications. Again, justify your assignments.

8. What is the structure of this passage? In other words, where is the Point positioned, and why?

1. <u>Arousal and Attraction</u> — Headline List

    1) Psychs D+A: how arousal → attractn
        — Wire bridge: aroused → attr.
    2) Expl: misattrib. physiol. effs AS attractn
        BUT actually <u>polarizn</u>: attr. OR repuls.   ← Point

2. The Point of the passage is in the last sentence of the second paragraph: *physiological arousal is reinterpreted as sexual attraction in the presence of an attractive partner, but as repulsion in the presence of an unattractive partner.* This message is labeled as *the true effect... probably.* The author is taking a little stand here. Everything in the passage leads up to this Point.

3. The first paragraph is all Background: facts are reported but not interpreted, as is necessary to support the Point. The second paragraph is Support, even though the cited theory of Dutton and Aron does not accord with the Point. Their theory is seen as simply an earlier version of a more sophisticated theory (that proposed by Foster and others).

4. The structure of the passage is Point Last, with Background and Support coming before it.

5. <u>Animal Treatment</u> — Headline List

    (1) 18th/e. 19th c.: Educ B's say animal cruelty = bad
    (2) Why: Part of broader embrace of compassn. Ex's   ← Point
    (3) Also: Industzn + urbanzn → concern for anims   ← Point
         — Nature romanticized

6. The Point here is complicated; it needs to be synthesized from the main ideas of the second and third paragraphs, together with some background from the first paragraph. The main message of the author can be written thus:

> *18th/19th c. British rejection of cruelty to animals stems from two factors: (1) broader embrace of compassion and (2) romanticization of nature by city dwellers.*

Thus, you need to note on your Headline list that both factors are part of the Point.

7. The first paragraph is Background. The rest of the passage is Support for the Point, split between the second and the third paragraphs.

8. The structure is Point in Middle. Background comes before, and Support comes after. What makes this structure a little more complicated in this case is that the Point is split among the topic sentences of two paragraphs (both of which are at the same level).

Chapter 4
of
READING COMPREHENSION

LONG
PASSAGES

In This Chapter . . .

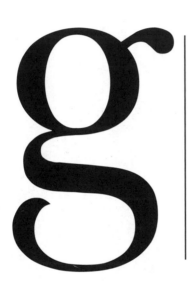

LONG PASSAGES: AN OVERVIEW

As noted in Chapter 1, long passages are more than 50 lines on the computer screen in length (or over 35 lines in the Official Guide). Long passages usually consist of four to five short paragraphs or three medium-length paragraphs, but they might consist of just two paragraphs. The word counts vary. The typical length is 325-375 words, but a few passages run 450-475 words.

You will generally see one long passage per GMAT exam, though you may see two. Each long passage will typically have four questions associated with it, although this may also vary.

Long passages present much the same challenge as short passages. All the issues presented by the computer delivery of the passage are the same. Although you can take a little more time to absorb a long passage, there is that much more to absorb. Thus, long and short passages are of roughly similar difficulty, all else being equal. If we accept the GMAT's claim that passages are ordered in *The Official Guide 12th Edition* by difficulty, then we see a slight correlation between length and difficulty. "Harder" passages in *The Official Guide* are slightly more likely to be long than short.

As discussed in the case of short passages, what really makes the difference between an "easy" or friendly passage and a "difficult" or unfriendly one is your background (*How much do you like this topic? What do you already know about this topic?*), as well as your status on the exam at that moment (*Are you ahead of pace or lagging behind? How are you feeling about how you are doing? How is your energy level, your focus, your processing speed?*).

If the long passage turns out to be friendly, then simply read it. Feel free to take any notes you like (indeed, it is a good habit to take notes every time), but you probably do not need to do so. You are off to the races with a passage you like and a brain that is firing on all cylinders.

On the other hand, when the passage is unfriendly (as many will probably be), you need a process you can count on. **You need a robust note-taking process** that you can carry out under any conditions, in order to read actively, rapidly, and effectively.

For a long passage, we will approach our notes slightly differently—by creating a SKELE-TAL SKETCH. As with the Headline List for short passages, a Skeletal Sketch serves several purposes:

(1) It fosters an understanding of the content and purpose of the passage by using writing to enable active reading.

(2) It provides a general structure without getting you bogged down in details.

(3) It promotes a fast first reading of a long, complex passage that still gives you enough time to answer questions.

The Skeletal Sketch emphasizes the first paragraph, or skull, and de-emphasizes the details contained in subsequent paragraphs.

The Skeletal Sketch

The creation of a Skeletal Sketch has several key elements:

1. The top of a skeleton (the skull) is its most defined feature. Likewise, the first paragraph of every long passage gives shape to the text. As such, **your Skeletal Sketch requires a defined "skull."**

The primary difference between a long passage and a short passage is that, with a long passage, the first paragraph is often substantially more important than the other paragraphs. Thus, you should take extra time to summarize the first paragraph, making sure that you thoroughly understand it.

To form the skull, read the first sentence of the first paragraph. Summarize it concisely on your scratch paper. Use the same notations and abbreviations as you do for Headline Lists of short passages.

Continue to read the first paragraph. As with short passages, you must decide how frequently you stop to take notes: after each sentence, after a couple of sentences, or after the entire paragraph. Again, the answer is that it depends on how well you are grasping the content and purpose of the text. The more difficult the passage, the more frequently you should stop to process what you have read.

In the skull, you should end up with notes on **every** sentence. After you have finished the first paragraph, mark the most important idea you have noted down. This is the main idea of the first paragraph.

2. The limbs of your Skeletal Sketch are short headlines or one-sentence summaries of each of the remaining paragraphs.

The subsequent paragraphs of a long passage are generally not as important as the first. As a result, you should read these paragraphs differently than you read the first paragraph.

Read each body paragraph to determine its main point or purpose. Focus on the first one or two sentences of the paragraph, since this is where the paragraph's topic is usually found.

Read the remaining sentences quickly, intentionally skimming over details and examples. There is no point in trying to absorb the nitty-gritty details in these sentences during this initial reading. If you are asked a question about a specific detail, you will need to reread these sentences anyway. In fact, it is often *counter-productive* to try to absorb these details, since doing so takes you away from the main goal of your initial reading and sketching.

That said, you must actually read everything. Be on the lookout for big surprises or important results. Sometimes, the GMAT buries such surprises or results within the body of a later paragraph, and you must be ready to add them to your Skeletal Sketch.

If you focus on constructing the simple story, then you will read with the appropriate level of attention: not too close, not too far away, but just right.

During your initial reading of the passage, identify the main idea of each body paragraph without getting bogged down in the details.

3. Once you have finished the passage, identify the Point.

After you have finished reading the passage and creating the Skeletal Sketch, glance back over your notes and over the passage. Make sure you know what the Point of the passage is. If it is not in your Skeletal Sketch already, be sure to add it. Then, label or mark the Point, so that you articulate it to yourself. This way, you are certain of the author's most important message. Now proceed to the first question.

Using Your Skeletal Sketch

How do you use your Skeletal Sketch to answer questions about the passage? The same way you use a Headline List for a short passage: you should avoid having to use it at all! The purpose of the Sketch is to facilitate your comprehension of the passage. You should be able to answer all GENERAL questions without referring either to your notes or to the passage.

As for SPECIFIC questions, you will need to find the details in the passage. You can often find these details on your own. But you can also use your Skeletal Sketch as a search tool.

Timing for Long Passages

Recall from our discussion of short passages the following rule to determine how much time to spend on a particular reading passage: **you have two minutes per question, total,** including time to read the passage, create a Skeletal Sketch, and answer all the questions.

Typically, each long passage has four questions associated with it. Thus, you have roughly **eight minutes** to read and sketch the long passage and then answer the associated questions.

Out of this eight-minute period, you should spend approximately 3.5 to 4 minutes reading and generating your Skeletal Sketch. Then you should spend between 60 and 70 seconds actually answering each question, taking more time for Specific questions and less time for General questions, as noted in the previous chapter.

You can best learn to create Skeletal Sketches by repeated practice. Study the model given at the end of this chapter, and do the In-Action exercises. Also create Skeletal Sketches of Official Guide passages as you practice later.

Spend approximately 8 minutes reading, creating a Skeletal Sketch, and answering all the questions for a given long passage.

Common Structures of Long Passages

Long passages often display one of the following three structures. These are essentially the same structures as for short passages, except that "Point First" means "Point in First Paragraph" and "Point Last" means "Point in Last Paragraph."

Point First	Point Last	(Point in Middle)
POINT *E.g.,* **X is true**	Background *E.g., Phenomenon Q happens*	Background *E.g., Phenomenon Q happens*
Support *Here's why*	Support *There is theory X There is theory Y Pros & cons*	**POINT** *Theory X explains Q*
(Optional Implications) *Here's what could result*	**POINT** *Theory X is better*	Support *Here's why* (Optional Implic.)

In a long passage, the first paragraph provides either the Point itself or background information crucial for understanding the Point.

Remember that the GMAT is not limited to these structures, especially if the Point is split up (i.e., the pieces are located in more than one place in the passage). Also remember that there is frequently foreshadowing.

Long passages often have more of a **narrative** to their simple story than short passages do. Here are three abstracted narratives contained within some long passages on the GMAT. Of course, there can be many others! Do NOT impose these narratives on every passage.

1. A Theory

　　Here is an area of scientific or historical **research**.
　　Here is a **theory** about that area of research.
　　Here is **support** for that theory.
　　(Possibly) Here are **implications** of that theory.
　　Point: EITHER the theory itself OR an assertion about the theory, e.g. **Theory X can now be tested**. In the latter case, support for the assertion is given.

2. A Couple of Theories

　　Here is a **phenomenon** in some area of scientific or historical research.
　　Here are a couple of **theories** about that phenomenon.
　　Here is **support** for each of those theories.
　　Point: **Theory X is best** OR **they all fall short**.

3. A Solution (rarer)

　　Here is a **problem** or a situation.
　　Point: I advocate this **solution** or this outcome.
　　Here is **support** for my position, and possibly **implications**.

Model Long Passage: *Electroconvulsive Therapy*

Electroconvulsive therapy (ECT) is a controversial psychiatric treatment involving the induction of a seizure in a patient by passing electricity through the brain. While beneficial effects of electrically induced seizures are evident and predictable in most patients, a unified mechanism of action has not yet been established and remains the subject of numerous investigations. ECT is extremely effective against severe depression, some acute psychotic states, and mania, though, like many other medical procedures, it has its risks.

Since the inception of ECT in 1938, the public has held a strongly negative conception of the procedure. Initially, doctors employed unmodified ECT. Patients were rendered instantly unconscious by the electrical current, but the strength of the muscle contractions from uncontrolled motor seizures often led to compression fractures of the spine or damage to the teeth. In addition to the effect this physical trauma had on public sentiment, graphic examples of abuse documented in books and movies, such as Ken Kesey's *One Flew Over the Cuckoo's Nest*, portrayed ECT as punitive, cruel, overused, and violative of patients' legal rights.

In comparison with its earlier incarnation, modern ECT is virtually unrecognizable. The treatment is modified by the muscle relaxant succinylcholine, which renders muscle contractions virtually nonexistent. Additionally, patients are given a general anesthetic. Thus, the patient is asleep and fully unaware during the procedure, and the only outward sign of a seizure may be the rhythmic movement of the patient's hand or foot. ECT is generally used in severely depressed patients for whom psychotherapy and medication prove ineffective. It may also be considered when there is an imminent risk of suicide, since antidepressants often require several weeks to show results. Exactly how ECT exerts its influence on behavior is not known, but repeated applications affect several important neurotransmitters in the brain, including serotonin, norepinephrine, and dopamine.

ECT has proven effective, but it remains controversial. Though decades-old studies showing brain cell death have been refuted in recent research, many patients do report loss of memory for events that occurred in the days, weeks or months surrounding the ECT. Some patients have also reported that their short-term memories continue to be affected for months after ECT, though some doctors argue that this memory malfunction may reflect the type of amnesia that sometimes results from severe depression.

By skimming over the details and thereby saving time, you should be able to read and sketch a long passage in roughly 3.5 to 4 minutes.

Turn the page to examine a model Skeletal Sketch.

Model Skeletal Sketch: *Electroconvulsive Therapy*

> 1) ECT = controv. psych. treat: Electr. into brain → seizure
> -- Beneficial, but mech not understood
> ** Very effective for some conditions; has risks
>
> 2) Since 1938, public dislikes ECT
>
> 3) Modern ECT totally diff
>
> 4) <u>ECT effective but still controv</u>   ← Point

The limbs of your sketch are concise one-line summaries of each body paragraph.

Notice that the "skull" of the sketch includes the most detail, as it carefully outlines the major points of the first paragraph.

The limbs of the sketch are each very concise, consisting only of a brief summary of the main idea of each body paragraph. Note that for each of the body paragraphs, the main idea is found in the first one or two sentences of the paragraph. This is often the case.

The Point of the passage is the first sentence of the last paragraph: *ECT has proven effective, but it remains controversial.* This is the most important message that the author wants to convey. Of course, we need the rest of the passage to supply context (e.g., to explain what ECT is in the first place). In fact, the last sentence of the first paragraph is very similar to the Point, but notice that *risks* are not quite the same thing as *controversy.*

The structure of this passage is Point Last (in the last paragraph). What comes before the Point is Background (explaining what ECT is) and Support, both for the controversial side of ECT (paragraph 2) and the effective side of ECT (paragraph 3).

Notice that the narrative here does NOT exactly fit one of the patterns mentioned earlier. The narrative here might best be expressed as "A Judgment about a Method": *Here is a method. It is effective but controversial.*

Problem Set

1. Read the following passage and create a Skeletal Sketch in 3.5-4 minutes. Afterward, using the sample given, critique your Skeletal Sketch by identifying ways in which it succeeds, as well as ways in which it could be improved.

Passage: Ether's Existence

In 1887, an ingenious experiment performed by Albert Michelson and Edward Morley severely undermined classical physics by failing to confirm the existence of "ether," a ghostly massless medium that was thought to permeate the universe. This finding had profound results, ultimately paving the way for acceptance of Einstein's special theory of relativity.

Prior to the Michelson–Morley experiment, nineteenth-century physics conceived of light as a wave propagated at constant speed through the ether. The existence of ether was hypothesized in part to explain the transmission of light, which was believed to be impossible through "empty" space. Physical objects, such as planets, were also thought to glide frictionlessly through the unmoving ether.

The Michelson–Morley experiment relied on the fact that the Earth, which orbits the Sun, would have to be in motion relative to a fixed ether. Just as a person on a motorcycle experiences a "wind" caused by her own motion relative to the air, the Earth would experience an "ethereal wind" caused by its motion through the ether. Such a wind would affect our measurements of the speed of light. If the speed of light is fixed with respect to the ether, but the earth is moving through the ether, then to an observer on Earth light must appear to move faster in a "downwind" direction than in an "upwind" direction.

In 1887 there were no clocks sufficiently precise to detect the speed differences that would result from an ethereal wind. Michelson and Morley surmounted this problem by using the wavelike properties of light itself to test for such speed differences. In their apparatus, known as an "interferometer", a single beam of light is split in half. Mirrors guide each half of the beam along a separate trajectory before ultimately reuniting the two half-beams into a single beam. If one half-beam has moved more slowly than the other, the reunited beams will be out of phase with each other. In other words, peaks of the first half-beam will not coincide exactly with peaks of the second half-beam, resulting in an interference pattern in the reunited beam. Michelson and Morley detected only a tiny degree of interference in the reunited light beam—far less than what was expected based on the motion of the Earth.

2. What is the Point of this passage? Justify your choice.

3. Identify the other components of the passage, if present: Background, Support, and Implications. Again, justify your assignments.

4. What is the structure of this passage? Where is the Point positioned, and why? What is the abstract narrative of this passage?

5. Read the following passage and create a Skeletal Sketch in 3.5–4 minutes. Afterward, using the sample given, critique your Skeletal Sketch by identifying ways in which it succeeds, as well as ways in which it could be improved.

Passage: Prescription Errors

In Europe, medical prescriptions were historically written in Latin, for many centuries the universal medium of communication among the educated. A prescription for eye drops written in Amsterdam could be filled in Paris, because the abbreviation *OS* meant "left eye" in both places. With the disappearance of Latin as a lingua franca, however, abbreviations such as *OS* can easily be confused with *AS* ("left ear") or *per os* ("by mouth"), even by trained professionals. Such misinterpretations of medical instructions can be fatal. In the early 1990s, two infants died in separate but identical tragedies: they were each administered 5 milligrams of morphine, rather than 0.5 milligrams, as the dosage was written without an initial zero. The naked decimal (.5) was subsequently misread.

The personal and economic costs of misinterpreted medical prescriptions and instructions are hard to quantify. However, anecdotal evidence suggests that misinterpretations are prevalent. While mistakes will always happen in any human endeavor, medical professionals, hospital administrators, and policymakers should continually work to drive the prescription error rate to zero, taking simple corrective steps and also pushing for additional investments.

Certain measures are widely agreed upon, even if some are difficult to enforce, given the decentralization of the country's healthcare system. For instance, the American Medical Association and other professional organizations have publicly advocated against the use of Latin abbreviations and other relics of historical pharmacology. As a result, incidents in which *qd* ("every day"), *qid* ("four times a day"), and *qod* ("every other day") have been mixed up seem to be on the decline. Other measures have been taken by regulators who oversee potential areas of confusion, such as drug names. For instance, the FDA asked a manufacturer to change the name of Levoxine, a thyroid medication, to Levoxyl, so that confusion with Lanoxin, a heart failure drug, would be reduced. Likewise, in 1990 the antacid Losec was renamed Prilosec at the FDA's behest to differentiate it from Lasix, a diuretic. Unfortunately, since 1992 there have been at least a dozen reports of accidental switches between Prilosec and Prozac, an antidepressant. As more drugs reach the market, drug-name "traffic control" will only become more complicated.

Other measures are controversial or require significant investment and consensus-building. For instance, putting the patient's condition on the prescription would allow double-checking but also reduce patient privacy; thus, this step continues to be debated. Computerized prescriber order entry (CPOE) systems seem to fix the infamous problem of illegible handwriting, but many CPOE systems permit naked decimals and other dangerous practices. Moreover, since fallible humans must still enter and retrieve the data, any technological fixes must be accompanied by substantial training. Ultimately, a multi-pronged approach is needed to address the issue.

6. What is the Point of this passage? Justify your choice.

7. Identify the other components of the passage, if present: Background, Support, and Implications. Again, justify your assignments.

8. What is the structure of this passage? Where is the Point positioned, and why? What is the abstract narrative of this passage?

1. <u>Ether's Existence</u> — Skeletal Sketch

> (1) 1887, <u>M+M experim. undermined class. physics</u>   ← Point
>   → No ether (ghostly medium thru-out univ)
>   — Profound result → accept E's thry rel
> (2) Before: light = wave in ether
> (3) M+M used Earth's motion in ether (like wind)
> (4)   → looked for speed diffs, found alm nothing

The "skull" of this sketch summarizes the brief first paragraph. The limbs are the summarized main ideas of each of the subsequent three paragraphs.

Notice that you have to pull more from the last paragraph than just the first sentence. You do not have to master how an interferometer works, but you have to have read everything in that last paragraph to get to the main idea, which is distributed throughout.

2. The Point of the passage is contained in the first sentence of the passage: *In 1887, an ingenious experiment performed by Albert Michelson and Edward Morley severely undermined classical physics by failing to confirm the existence of "ether,"*…. (Of course, you should not copy this word for word into your Skeletal Sketch, but instead abbreviate it dramatically, as is shown above.) Everything else in this passage is secondary to this assertion.

3. The first paragraph gives Background on the ether (*a ghostly massless medium that was thought to permeate the universe*) and also gives an Implication (*This finding had profound results… theory of relativity*). The rest of the passage is a combination of Background knowledge and Support for the assertion made in the Point.

4. The structure of the passage is Point First. In fact, the Point is the very first sentence. By placing the Point first in this passage, the author plants a stake in the ground, asserting the importance of the topic from the get-go (*…severely undermined classical physics…*) and providing the reader a sense of direction necessary for such a technical topic that requires a lot of Background. The narrative might be called "An Experiment": *M+M's shook physics, paved the way for Einstein. Here is what people used to think existed. Here is what M+M did to look. Here is what they found: Nothing!*

5. <u>Prescription Errors</u> — Skeletal Sketch

> (1) Eur: Rx in Latin, educ. Same in G, F.
>   BUT now easy to confuse abbrev.
>   — Can be fatal. Ex: 2 babies.
> (2) Cost Rx mistakes = hard to quant, but prevalent
>   Med prof, admin, pol should elim errors   ← Point
> (3) Some steps = agreed.
> (4) Other steps harder. Need multi-prong.

Incidentally, Rx is an abbreviation for "prescription," probably originating from Latin. If you happen to encounter a passage on prescription drugs, feel free to use this abbreviation; otherwise, use it to locate a pharmacy when traveling abroad.

6. The Point is the last sentence of the second paragraph: *While mistakes will always happen in any human endeavor, medical professionals, hospital administrators, and policymakers should continually work to drive the prescription error rate to zero, taking simple corrective steps and also pushing for additional investments.* This is the strongest and most general claim made by the author.

7. What comes before the Point is a mixture of Background (e.g., the use of Latin on medieval prescriptions) and Support (e.g., the explanation of the fatal tragedies). After the Point is mostly Implications (various potential steps with pros and cons). The last two paragraphs could be interpreted as judgments on specific tactics, *given* that we all want to drive the error rate down to zero.

8. The structure is Point in Middle. The Point may be positioned in the middle because the author wants to set up the Point with Background and Support stories first, generating outrage about the infant deaths. Then he or she can assert the Point, which does not require much more subsequent support.

Chapter 5
of
READING COMPREHENSION

THE SEVEN
STRATEGIES

In This Chapter . . .

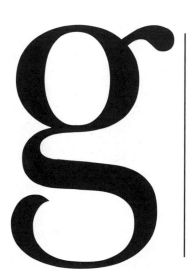

- General Questions: Scoring System Strategy
- Specific Questions: Key Word Strategy
- Specific Questions: Proof Sentence Strategy
- Justification Strategy
- Extreme Word Strategy
- Inference Strategy
- Preview Strategy

QUESTION TYPES

As discussed earlier, GMAT Reading Comprehension questions come in a variety of forms, but they can be placed into two major categories:

  (1) GENERAL questions
  (2) SPECIFIC questions

In this chapter, you will learn Seven Strategies for answering Reading Comprehension questions. The first of these strategies will help you answer General questions. The second and third strategies will help you answer Specific questions. The last four strategies are applicable to both General and Specific questions.

General Questions

General questions deal with the main idea, purpose, organization, and structure of a passage. Typical general questions are phrased as follows:

  The primary purpose of the passage is...?
  The main idea of the passage is...?
  Which of the following best describes the organization of the passage?
  The passage as a whole can best be characterized as which of the following?

The correct answer to general questions such as *What is the main idea of this passage?* should relate to as much of the passage as possible.

Your understanding of the passage gained through generating a Headline List or a Skeletal Sketch provides the key to answering general questions. You should be able to answer general questions without having to reread the entire passage. In fact, rereading the entire passage can actually be distracting. An incorrect answer choice may pertain only to a detail in a body paragraph. As you reread, you might spot that attractive detail and choose the wrong answer.

So, instead of rereading, **dive right into the answer choices and start eliminating.** If you need to, **review the Point** so that you are certain in your knowledge of the author's main message. Armed with the Point, you should be able to eliminate two or three choices quickly.

The last four strategies described in this chapter will help you get to the final answer. Occasionally, though, you may still find yourself stuck between two answer choices on a general question. If this is the case, use a Scoring System to determine which answer choice relates to more paragraphs in the passage. Assign the answer choice two points if it relates to the first paragraph. Give one more point for each additional related paragraph. The answer choice with more points is usually the correct one. In the event of a tie, select the answer choice that pertains to the first paragraph over any choices that do not.

> **STRATEGY for GENERAL Q's: If you are stuck between two answer choices, use a SCORING SYSTEM to assign a value to each one.**

General questions can often be answered without having to reread the entire passage.

*Manhattan*GMAT*Prep
the new standard

Specific Questions

Specific questions deal with details, inferences, assumptions, and arguments. Typical specific questions are phrased as follows:

> According to the passage...?
> It can be inferred from the passage that...?
> All of the following statements are supported by the passage EXCEPT...?
> Which of the following is an assumption underlying the statement that...?

In contrast to your approach to General questions, you will need to reread and grasp details in the passage to answer Specific questions. First, read the question and focus on the key words you are most likely to find in the passage. Then, look back over the passage to find those key words. Use your Headline List or Skeletal Sketch as a search tool, if necessary. Do NOT look at the answer choices. Four out of five of them are meant to mislead you.

> **STRATEGY for SPECIFIC Q's: Identify the KEY WORDS in the question. Then, go back to the passage and find those key words.**

Use the structure provided by your Headline List or Skeletal Sketch to help decide which paragraph contains the correct answer.

Consider the limbs of the sample Skeletal Sketch below:

1) Standardized tests = not valid predict.
2) Timing test implies → "fast = smart" BUT not true
3) Tests = also biased ag. non-native spkrs

Imagine that you are presented with this question: *Robinson raises the issue of cultural bias to do which of the following?* You would start scanning the passage looking for *cultural bias*. Since you just created the sketch, you would probably head toward the third paragraph anyway, but if necessary, the sketch would remind you to look there.

Sometimes, you will need to find a synonym for the key words in the question. For example, if the question addresses *weapons of mass destruction*, you may need to find a paragraph that addresses *nuclear* or *chemical* or *biological weapons*.

Once you find the key words, you should reread the surrounding sentence or sentences to answer the question. You may have to do a little thought work or take a few notes to figure out what the sentences exactly mean. That is expected: after all, you did not master those details the first time through. In fact, do not look at the answer choices until you **boil down the relevant sentence or sentences into a "mantra"**—five words of truth. Then you can bring back that mantra and hold it in your head as you scan the five answer choices, eliminating the four lies and matching your mantra to the truth.

> **STRATEGY for SPECIFIC Q's: Find one or two PROOF SENTENCES to defend the correct answer choice.**

Only a handful of specific questions require more than two proof sentences.

Strategies for All Reading Comprehension Questions

You should implement the following strategies for all Reading Comprehension questions.

> ### STRATEGY: JUSTIFY every word in the answer choice.

In the correct answer choice, **every word must be completely true** and within the scope of the passage. If you cannot justify *every* word in the answer choice, eliminate it. For example, consider the answer choices below:

(A) The colonists resented the king for taxing them without representation.
(B) England's policy of taxation without representation caused resentment among the colonists.

The difference in these two answer choices lies in the word *king* versus the word *England*. Although this seems like a small difference, it is the key to eliminating one of these answer choices. If the passage does not mention the *king* when it discusses the colonists' resentment, then the word *king* cannot be justified, and the answer choice should be eliminated.

One word can render an otherwise acceptable answer choice incorrect.

> ### STRATEGY: AVOID extreme words if possible.

Avoid Reading Comprehension answer choices that use extreme words. These words, such as *all* and *never,* tend to broaden the scope of an answer choice too much or make it too extreme. **The GMAT prefers moderate language and ideas**. Eliminate answer choices that go too far. Of course, occasionally you are justified in picking an extreme choice, but the passage must back you up 100%.

> ### STRATEGY: INFER as little as possible.

Many Reading Comprehension questions ask you to infer something from the passage. An inference is an informed deduction. Reading Comprehension inferences rarely go far beyond what is stated in the passage. In general, you should infer so little that the inference seems obvious. It is often surprising how simplistic GMAT inferences are. If an answer choice answers the question AND can be confirmed by language in the passage, it will be the correct one. Conversely, you should eliminate answer choices that require any logical stretch or leap. When you read *The passage suggests…* or *The passage implies…*, you should rephrase that language: *The passage STATES JUST A LITTLE DIFFERENTLY…* . **You must be able to prove the answer, just as if the question asked you to look it up in the passage**.

You should think the same way on Critical Reasoning problems. For instance, when you Draw a Conclusion, go with what you can *prove* from what you are given. On both Reading Comprehension and Critical Reasoning, stick with the words on the screen!

STRATEGY: PREVIEW the first question.

As you read through a passage for the first time and create a Headline List or Skeletal Sketch, you will not know all of the questions that you will have to answer on that passage, since the questions appear on the computer screen one at a time. However, you will know the first question, since it appears on the screen at the same time as the passage.

You may want to read this question before reading the passage, so that you can have one question in the back of your mind while you read and sketch. Most of the time, this first question will be a General question (e.g., *What is the purpose of the passage?*). Occasionally, however, it will be a Specific question that focuses on a particular detail. Knowing the question before you read can help you to spot that detail and save time later.

The first question on a reading passage is typically, though not always, a General question.

The Seven Strategies for Reading Comprehension

You now have seven effective strategies to use on Reading Comprehension questions on the GMAT. Make sure that you know them and practice them frequently.

For GENERAL questions:

(1) Use a **SCORING SYSTEM** when stuck between two answer choices.

For SPECIFIC questions:

(2) Match **KEY WORDS** in specific questions to key words (or synonyms) in the passage.

(3) Defend your answer choice with one or two **PROOF SENTENCES**.

For ALL questions:

(4) **JUSTIFY** every word in your answer choice.

(5) Avoid answer choices that contain **EXTREME** words.

(6) Choose an answer choice that **INFERS** as **LITTLE** as possible.

And do not forget to:

(7) **PREVIEW** the first question before reading the passage.

Practice using the 7 strategies on the Problem Set in the last chapter of this book.

Chapter 6
of
READING COMPREHENSION

QUESTION
ANALYSIS

In This Chapter . . .

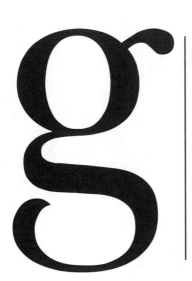

QUESTION TYPE ANALYSIS

As you begin a Reading Comprehension question, you should classify it right away as General or Specific. This distinction determines your fundamental approach to the question. With General questions, you dive right into eliminating answer choices, but with Specific questions, you go back to the passage and find proof sentences before looking at the answer choices.

That said, we can break down each type into a few common subtypes as follows. You should not spend any time classifying questions into these subtypes. We provide this further classification simply so that you can become more familiar with the variety of possible questions on the GMAT.

General Questions

    (a) Main Idea: *The primary purpose of the passage is...*

    (b) Organization: *The function of the third paragraph is...*

    (c) Tone: *The tone of the passage can be best described as...*

Specific Questions

    (a) Lookup: *According to the passage, the Ojibway used cowry shells as...*

    (b) Inference: *The passage suggests that computer magazines have survived because...* As mentioned earlier, despite the "inference" language of these questions, you must treat these questions like Lookups. That is, you must go back to the passage, find proof sentences, and prove your answer. You should infer as little as possible.

    (c) Minor types (Organization and Tone can have a specific focus; also, you might be asked to Strengthen or Weaken an assertion in the passage)

In addition, any of these question types could include an "EXCEPT," which would make the phrasing more complicated. For instance, a Specific Lookup question could read *According to the passage, all of the following are functions of bone marrow EXCEPT....*

Types of Wrong Answer Choices

Wrong answers on Reading Comprehension questions tend to fall into one of five broad categories. Caution: you should generally NOT try to classify wrong answers right away. You should not waste precious time or attention classifying an answer choice that is obviously wrong. Rather, use this classification in the last stage of elimination, if you are stuck deciding among answer choices that all seem attractive.

This classification originates from an in-depth analysis of the questions published in *The Official Guide* (*12th Edition* and *Verbal Review*). The proportions listed correspond to the proportion of Official Guide answer choices that fall into the different categories.

The best way to familiarize yourself with the variety of Reading Comprehension question types is to answer real practice questions found in *The Official Guide for GMAT Review.*

1. Out of Scope (40–50% of wrong answers in the Official Guide)
- **Introduces an unwarranted assertion** supported nowhere in the passage.
- Might be "Real-World Plausible." That is, the answer might be true or seem to be true in the real world. However, if the answer is not supported in the passage, it is out of scope.
- Found in all question types, though less often in Specific Lookup questions.

2. Direct Contradiction (20–25% of wrong answers)
- **States the exact opposite** of something asserted in the passage.
- Paradoxically attractive, because it relates to the passage closely. If you miss one contrast or switchback in the trail, you can easily think a Direct Contradiction is the right answer.
- Found in all question types, but less often in General questions.

Incorrect answer choices
come in different vari-
eties that you should
recognize.

3. Mix-Up (10–15% of wrong answers)
- **Scrambles together disparate content** from the passage.
- Tries to trap the student who simply matches language, not meaning.
- Found more often in Specific questions.

4. One Word Wrong (10–15% of wrong answers)
- **Just one word (or maybe 2) is incorrect**. Includes extreme words.
- More prevalent in General questions.

5. True But Irrelevant (~10% of wrong answers)
- True according to the passage, but does not answer the given question.
- May be too narrow or simply unrelated.
- More prevalent in General questions.

This framework can be particularly helpful as you analyze the patterns in wrong answers that you incorrectly choose during practice (whether under exam-like conditions or not). If you frequently choose Direct Contradiction answers, for instance, then you might incorporate one more double-check into your process to look for that particular sort of error. Again, however, **you should not attempt to classify wrong answers as a first line of attack**. This strategy is inefficient and even distracting.

In the rest of this chapter, we will review two of the passages used as examples in the previous chapters covering short and long passages.

Note: For the purpose of practice and exposure to different question types, we will be reviewing four questions on the short passage and five questions on the long passage. However, on the GMAT, a short passage will typically have only three questions associated with it, and a long passage will typically have only four questions associated with it.

Reread the first passage, reproduced on the following page for your convenience. As you read, create a Headline List. Do not try to reproduce the earlier version; simply make your own. On the pages that follow, try to answer each question in the appropriate amount of time (between 60 and 90 seconds) BEFORE you read the accompanying explanation.

Model Short Passage Revisited: *Insect Behavior*

Insect behavior generally appears to be explicable in terms of unconscious stimulus-response mechanisms; when scrutinized, it often reveals a stereotyped, inflexible quality. A classic example is the behavior of the female sphex wasp. In a typical case, the mother leaves her egg sealed in a burrow alongside a paralyzed grasshopper, which her larva can eat when it hatches. Before she deposits the grasshopper in the burrow, she leaves it at the entrance and goes inside to inspect the burrow. If the inspection reveals no problems, she drags the grasshopper inside by its antennae. Scientific experiments have uncovered an inability on the wasp's part to change its behavior when experiencing disruptions of this routine.

Charles Darwin discovered that if the grasshopper's antennae are removed the wasp will not drag it into the burrow, even though the legs or ovipositor could serve the same function as the antennae. Later Jean-Henri Fabre found more evidence of the wasp's dependence on predetermined routine. While a wasp was performing her inspection of a burrow, he moved the grasshopper a few centimeters away from the burrow's mouth. The wasp brought the grasshopper back to the edge of the burrow, then began a whole new inspection. When Fabre took this opportunity to move the food again, the wasp repeated her routine. Fabre performed his disruptive maneuver forty times, and the wasp's response never changed.

Review the model passage and recreate the Headline List. Try to answer the questions that follow before reading the explanations.

Your Headline List:

1. The primary purpose of the passage is to _____.

(A) prove, based on examples, that insects lack consciousness
(B) argue that insects are unique in their dependence on rigid routines
(C) analyze the maternal behavior of wasps
(D) compare and contrast the work of Darwin and Fabre
(E) argue that insect behavior relies on rigid routines which appear to be unconscious

---

Even if one answer choice looks promising, always review all of the answer choices before making a selection.

This is a GENERAL question (subtype: Main Idea), so we should be able to answer the question using the understanding of the passage that we gained through creating our Headline List. For questions asking about the main idea of the passage, be sure to refer to the opening paragraph, which either articulates the Point of the passage or sets up the necessary context.

We can eliminate (A) based upon the topic sentence in the first paragraph. The passage does not claim to prove that insects lack consciousness; it merely suggests, rather tentatively, that insect behavior *appears to be explicable* in terms of unconscious mechanisms. The word *prove* is too extreme in answer choice (A). [One Word Wrong]

Answer choice (B) reflects the language of the passage in that the passage does indicate that insects depend on rigid routines. However, it does not address the question of whether there are any other animals that depend on such routines, as is stated in answer choice (B). The passage makes no claim about whether or not insects are *unique* in this respect. Remember that every word in an answer choice must be justified from the text. [Out of Scope]

We can eliminate answer choice (C) using our Headline List. It is clear that the sphex wasp's maternal behavior is used as an example to illustrate a more general idea; this behavior is not itself the Point of the passage. [True But Irrelevant]

The fact that Fabre and Darwin only appear in the second paragraph is a good indication that they are not the passage's primary concern. Fabre and Darwin are simply mentioned as sources for some of the information on wasps. Moreover, their results are not contrasted; rather, their experiments are both cited as evidence to support the Point. Answer choice (D) is incorrect. [Out of Scope]

(E) CORRECT. The passage begins with a topic sentence that announces the author's Point. The Point has two parts, as this answer choice correctly indicates: (1) insect behavior relies on rigid routines, and (2) these routines appear to be unconscious. The topic sentence does not use the term *rigid routine*, but it conveys the idea of rigidity by describing insect behavior as *inflexible*. The concept of routine is introduced later in the passage.

As is typical on the GMAT, the correct answer choice avoids restating the passage. Instead, this choice uses synonyms (e.g. *rigid* instead of *inflexible*).

2. **The second paragraph performs which of the following functions in the passage?**

(A) It provides experimental evidence of the inflexibility of one kind of insect behavior.
(B) It contradicts the conventional wisdom about "typical" wasp behavior.
(C) It illustrates the strength of the wasp's maternal affection.
(D) It explores the logical implications of the thesis articulated in the first paragraph.
(E) It highlights historical changes in the conduct of scientific research.

Questions that ask about the structure of a passage are GENERAL questions (subtype: Organization). We should be able to answer the question using the understanding of the passage that we gained through creating our Headline List.

If we use our model Headline List, we see that the main ideas of the second paragraph are as follows:

2) D: wasp won't drag g. w/o anten.
   F: similar evid

The second paragraph describes experiments that are used as examples of inflexible insect behavior. This concept is mirrored closely in answer choice **(A)**, the correct answer.

We should always review all answer choices, as more than one may be promising.

We can eliminate answer choice **(B)**. The passage does not mention any challenge to a conventional view; for all we know, the passage simply states the mainstream scientific position on insect behavior. [Out of Scope]

For answer choice **(C)** it might be tempting to infer that the wasp's persistence is caused by maternal affection. This inference is questionable, however, because the passage states that insect behavior is determined by mechanistic routines which appear to be unemotional in nature. Always avoid picking an answer choice that depends on a debatable inference, because the correct answer should not stray far from what is directly stated in the text. [Out of Scope]

Choice **(D)** is incorrect because Darwin's and Fabre's experiments do not explore the logical <u>implications</u> of the idea that insect behavior is inflexible. Rather, the experiments are presented as <u>evidence</u> of inflexibility. [Direct Contradiction]

Answer choice **(E)** goes beyond the scope of the passage. The paragraph mentions work by two scientists, but it does not tell us whether any differences in their methods were part of a historical change in the conduct of science. [Out of Scope]

You should be able to justify every word in the answer choice that you select.

*Manhattan*GMAT*Prep

3. The passage mentions the grasshopper's ovipositor in the second paragraph in order to

(A) shed light on an anatomical peculiarity of grasshoppers
(B) illustrate the wasp's inability to avail itself of alternative methods
(C) provide a scientific synonym for the word "leg"
(D) invoke Darwin's theory of functional evolution
(E) concede that a grasshopper becomes more difficult to move when its antennae are removed

The correct answer will NOT require the use of outside knowledge, so eliminate any answer choice that does.

This is a SPECIFIC question that requires an understanding of the purpose of a specific detail in the passage. Thus, the subtype of the question is Inference, since we may not be given an explicit reason for the inclusion of the detail.

The first step in answering this question is to find the word *ovipositor* in the passage and reread the surrounding sentence or sentences. The question stem helpfully directs us to the second paragraph. We can quickly find the term *ovipositor* in the first sentence of that paragraph:

> Charles Darwin discovered that if the grasshopper's antennae are removed the wasp will not drag it into the burrow, even though the legs or ovipositor could serve the same function as the antennae.

We should use this sentence to justify the correct answer choice.

Answer choice (**A**) can be eliminated, as the sentence and the passage give us no anatomical information about grasshoppers. We are not told whether an ovipositor is a peculiarity of grasshoppers. [Out of Scope]

Answer choice (**B**) is related directly to the substance of our proof sentence. The ovipositor is mentioned as an alternative to the grasshopper's antennae that the wasp could have used to drag the grasshopper. Though this answer choice is a strong candidate for the correct choice, we should remember to review all answer choices, as sometimes more than one can seem correct, forcing us to distinguish between two answer choices more closely.

Answer choice (**C**) may be considered tempting. Perhaps the passage mentions the ovipositor as a technical term for a grasshopper leg. However, a number of technical clues tell us that *ovipositor* is not being presented as a synonym for *leg*:

(1) The passage reads *the legs* [plural] *or ovipositor*, so we know *ovipositor* is not being presented as a synonym for *leg* (singular).
(2) The words *or ovipositor* are not set off with commas, as in "the leg, or ovipositor," which would be the normal way of indicating that one word is a synonym for another.
(3) *Ovipositor* is a difficult word. Normally the text would provide an easy synonym after a hard word, as in "the ovipositor, or leg," not the other way around.

The passage's actual phrasing (*the legs or ovipositor*) clearly indicates <u>two separate parts</u> of the grasshopper's anatomy. Answer choice (**C**) is incorrect. [Mix-Up]

Answer choice (**D**) tries to tempt you by using assumed background knowledge. When you see the name *Darwin*, you probably immediately think of Darwin's theory of evolution. On the GMAT, any answer choice that requires outside knowledge will generally be incorrect. The passage never mentions the theory of evolution, so we should eliminate answer choice (**D**). [Out of Scope]

The words *even though the legs or ovipositor could serve the same function as the antennae* in our proof sentence indicate that using the legs or ovipositor would be <u>no more difficult</u> for the wasp than using the antennae to drag the grasshopper. We can eliminate answer choice (**E**) for this reason. [Direct Contradiction]

Thus, the correct answer to this problem is answer choice (**B**).

Note: To answer this question, you do not need to know what *ovipositor* means. You just need to understand the logic of the sentence and the passage in which the word appears. But in case you are curious, an ovipositor is a tubular organ through which a female insect or fish deposits her eggs.

> Stick closely to the language of the passage. Avoid any answer choices that go too far beyond that language.

---

4. The passage supports which of the following statements about insect behavior?

(A) Reptiles such as snakes behave more flexibly than do insects.
(B) Insects such as honeybees can always be expected to behave inflexibly.
(C) Many species of insects leave eggs alongside living but paralyzed food sources.
(D) Stimulus-response mechanisms in insects have evolved because, under ordinary circumstances, they help insects to survive.
(E) More than one species of insect displays inflexible, routine behaviors.

This is a difficult SPECIFIC question (subtype: Lookup). The key words *insect behavior* indicate the topic of the passage; they could plausibly refer to almost anything mentioned. Thus, we must change tactics and start with the answer choices. Each answer choice gives us additional key words; we use these to look up the reference for each answer choice and determine whether the choice is justified.

The key to finding the correct answer is to focus on what is explicitly stated in the passage, and to examine whether each answer choice goes beyond what can be supported by the passage. Here, our Headline List and our understanding of the structure of the passage would direct us to the first paragraph. Again, justify every word in the answer choice that you select.

Answer choice **(A)** mentions reptiles and snakes. Since the passage never mentions either of these, you should eliminate this answer choice. This is the case even though one could argue that the passage draws an implicit contrast between insect inflexibility and the more flexible behavior of some other creatures. You should discard any answer choice that goes too far beyond the passage. [Out of Scope]

Answer choice **(B)** is a great example of a tempting GMAT answer choice. Honeybees are insects, and the passage does claim that insect behavior tends to be inflexible. However, the passage does not say that every single species of insect behaves inflexibly; perhaps honeybees are an exception. Further, this answer choice states that honeybees *always* behave inflexibly, whereas the author states that insect behavior *often* *reveals a stereotyped, inflexible quality*. The extreme word *always* cannot be justified in this answer choice. [One Word Wrong]

Extreme words are not always wrong in answer choices. However, any extreme words must be clearly justified by the passage.

Answer choice **(C)** seems plausible. The sphex wasp is probably not the only species of insect that provides its young with paralyzed prey. However, the word *Many* is not justified in the passage. We do not know the behavior of any other insect in this regard. Through the use of the word *Many*, answer choice **(C)** goes too far beyond the passage. [One Word Wrong]

The passage never explicitly mentions evolution, nor does it make any statement about why insects have stimulus-response mechanisms. Answer choice **(D)** also requires drawing inferences from beyond the text of the passage. [Out of Scope]

The first sentence of the passage tells us that *Insect behavior generally appears to be explicable in terms of unconscious stimulus-response mechanisms* and *often reveals a stereotyped, inflexible quality.* The passage goes on to describe the case of sphex wasps as a *classic example.* Thus, the passage clearly indicates that the case of sphex wasps is not completely unique; that is, there must be more than one species of insect that exhibits inflexible behavior. Note that *more than one* can be justified by the passage in a way that a more extreme term such as *most* or *all* cannot be. Answer choice **(E)** is correct.

Now reread the Model Long Passage, reproduced on the following page for your convenience. As you read, create a Skeletal Sketch. Do not try to reproduce the earlier version; simply make your own. On the pages that follow, try to answer each question in the appropriate amount of time (between 60 and 90 seconds) BEFORE you read the accompanying explanation.

Model Long Passage Revisited: *Electroconvulsive Therapy*

Electroconvulsive therapy (ECT) is a controversial psychiatric treatment involving the induction of a seizure in a patient by passing electricity through the brain. While beneficial effects of electrically induced seizures are evident and predictable in most patients, a unified mechanism of action has not yet been established and remains the subject of numerous investigations. ECT is extremely effective against severe depression, some acute psychotic states, and mania, though, like many medical procedures, it has its risks.

Since the inception of ECT in 1938, the public has held a strongly negative conception of the procedure. Initially, doctors employed unmodified ECT. Patients were rendered instantly unconscious by the electrical current, but the strength of the muscle contractions from uncontrolled motor seizures often led to compression fractures of the spine or damage to the teeth. In addition to the effect this physical trauma had on public sentiment, graphic examples of abuse documented in books and movies, such as Ken Kesey's *One Flew Over the Cuckoo's Nest*, portrayed ECT as punitive, cruel, overused, and violative of patients' legal rights.

Modern ECT is virtually unrecognizable from its earlier days. The treatment is modified by the muscle relaxant succinylcholine, which renders muscle contractions virtually nonexistent. Additionally, patients are given a general anesthetic. Thus, the patient is asleep and fully unaware during the procedure, and the only outward sign of a seizure may be the rhythmic movement of the patient's hand or foot. ECT is generally used in severely depressed patients for whom psychotherapy and medication prove ineffective. It may also be considered when there is an imminent risk of suicide, since antidepressants often take several weeks to work effectively. Exactly how ECT exerts its effects is not known, but repeated applications affect several neurotransmitters in the brain, including serotonin, norepinephrine, and dopamine.

ECT has proven effective, but it is not without controversy. Though decades-old studies showing brain cell death have been refuted in recent research, many patients do report loss of memory for events that occurred in the days, weeks or months surrounding the ECT. Some patients have also reported that their short-term memories continue to be affected for months after ECT, though some doctors argue that this memory malfunction may reflect the type of amnesia that sometimes results from severe depression.

Do not try to get all the details down in your Skeletal Sketch. Just focus on the simple story and the structure of the passage.

Your Skeletal Sketch:

1. The passage is primarily concerned with

(A) defending a provocative medical practice
(B) explaining a controversial medical treatment
(C) arguing for further testing of a certain medical approach
(D) summarizing recent research concerning a particular medical procedure
(E) relating the public concern toward a particular medical therapy

---

This is a GENERAL question (subtype: Main Idea). It asks for the primary purpose of the passage, although the question is worded slightly differently. We should be able to answer this question relying upon the comprehension of the passage that we gained through creating our Skeletal Sketch.

The answer to a question about the primary concern of a passage should reflect our understanding of the Point. As we noted before, the Point of this passage is the topic sentence of the fourth paragraph: *ECT has proven effective, but it is not without controversy.* This Point is neutral and balanced; it is not advocating either the adoption or the elimination of ECT.

Answer choice (**A**) states that the passage explicitly *defends* ECT. The passage addresses ECT in an objective manner; the author neither defends nor argues against the continued use of ECT as a viable medical therapy. Answer choice (**A**) is incorrect. [One Word Wrong]

Answer choice (**B**) is correct. The primary purpose of the passage is to explain ECT. This includes briefly discussing both its purpose and the reasons why it has generated such controversy. This answer choice is reflected in our Skeletal Sketch and in our grasp of the Point.

We should continue to rule out other answer choices.

Answer choice (**C**) describes a need for further testing that is never mentioned in the passage. You might think that the passage implies this need, since we do not know *exactly how ECT exerts its effects,* for instance. However, the primary concern of the passage will not simply be implied; it will be asserted. Answer choice (**C**) is incorrect. [Out of Scope]

Although recent research concerning a particular side effect of ECT is mentioned in the final paragraph, this is not the primary purpose of the passage. This answer choice is too specific for a primary purpose question. It does not relate to the content of the passage as a whole. Using the scoring system strategy, you would give this answer choice only one point since it relates to the final paragraph. In contrast, the correct answer choice (B) would be assigned 5 points since it relates to the first paragraph (2 points) and each of the subsequent 3 paragraphs (1 point each). Answer choice (**D**) is incorrect. [True But Irrelevant]

The passage does state that ECT is a controversial procedure that the public views in a negative manner; however, the passage only focuses on public concern over the procedure in the second paragraph. This answer choice is too specific for a primary purpose question, and does not encompass the majority of the passage. Using the point system strategy, this answer choice would receive only one point since it relates to only the second paragraph. Thus, answer choice (**E**) is also incorrect. [True But Irrelevant]

2. Which of the following is NOT cited in the passage as a current or historical criticism of ECT?

(A) ECT causes the death of brain cells.
(B) ECT has been used to punish certain individuals.
(C) Seizures during ECT can cause bodily harm.
(D) Short-term memory loss results from ECT.
(E) Repeated applications of ECT affect several neurotransmitters in the brain.

This SPECIFIC question (subtype: Lookup) asks us which criticism of ECT is NOT cited in the passage. A methodical process of elimination is the best approach to answer a "NOT" or "EXCEPT" question. Use your understanding of the passage to locate the important information in the passage. If necessary, refer to your Skeletal Sketch. Then eliminate each answer choice as soon as you prove that it *is* cited as a criticism of ECT.

The second sentence of the final paragraph indicates that the death of brain cells was the basis for an historical criticism of ECT. Although the research was recently refuted, brain cell death is still a side-effect that, at one time, caused criticism of the procedure. Answer choice **(A)** can be ruled out.

According to the final sentence of the second paragraph, one reason why the public has a negative perception of ECT is that certain uses (or abuses) of ECT have been *documented in books and movies.* The word *documented* means that these abuses actually happened. Moreover, these abuses have been documented as *punitive;* in other words, ECT has been used to punish people. Thus, answer choice **(B)** can be eliminated.

The second paragraph explicitly and prominently mentions the bodily harm caused by seizures during unmodified ECT in its second and third sentences. Answer choice **(C)** is clearly incorrect.

The second sentence of the final paragraph also cites short term memory loss as the primary reason that ECT, in its current modified form, still generates controversy. Thus, answer choice **(D)** is incorrect.

The end of the third paragraph specifically states that *repeated applications [of ECT] affect several neurotransmitters in the brain.* However, this statement is offered in a neutral way, not as a criticism of ECT, but simply as additional information about the procedure. You might suppose that this effect is negative, but the text itself does not apply a judgment one way or the other. Answer choice **(E)** is the only answer choice that is not cited as a past or current criticism of ECT. Therefore answer choice **(E)** is the correct answer.

With a "NOT" or "EXCEPT" question, it is often easier to eliminate incorrect answer choices than to identify the correct answer choice directly. Also, the GMAT has a tendency to make the correct answer (D) or (E) on "EXCEPT" questions, to force you to read all of the answer choices. Thus, you may want to start with the last answer choice and work your way up, for this sort of question.

With a "NOT" or "EXCEPT" question, you should use a methodical process of elimination.

3. The tone of the passage suggests that the author regards ECT with

(A) conditional support
(B) academic objectivity
(C) mild advocacy
(D) unreserved criticism
(E) increasing acceptance

Tone questions are General questions, but they often require a second look at the specific word choices in the passage.

This is a GENERAL question (subtype: Tone). Although you can often answer a Tone question using only your general understanding of the passage, you should still closely examine the specific words the author uses to convey information. Here, the author presents evidence both for and against the efficacy and safety of ECT; he or she does not clearly lean toward or against more widespread adoption of the treatment. When presenting criticisms of ECT, the author does so in a manner that does not indicate a clear bias. The correct answer will reflect this balance.

Also, note that when answer choices are only two words long, the wrong answers will be wrong by just one or two words! Thus, all the incorrect answers below are One Word Wrong.

Answer choice **(A)** is incorrect, as the author's tone does not indicate support for ECT. Moreover, there are no clear conditions placed upon any support by the author.

Answer choice **(B)** is the correct answer. The tone of the passage is impartial and objective. The passage explains the history and discussion of ECT in an unbiased, academic manner. We should still continue to examine all answer choices.

Answer choice **(C)** is incorrect, as the tone of the passage does not suggest even mild advocacy on the part of the author. Though the author admits the *proven* efficacy of ECT, this admission is counterbalanced by accounts of criticisms and controversy surrounding the treatment. The tone of the passage is not supportive overall.

Answer choice **(D)** is incorrect, as the language is too extreme. The tone of the passage is not unreserved, and the author is not clearly critical in his stance toward ECT.

Answer choice **(E)** is also not an accurate representation of the tone of the passage. It may be the case that ECT has achieved growing acceptance since its inception, but this reflects the popular or medical perception, not that of the author.

4. Which of the following can be inferred from the third paragraph?

(A) Greater amounts of the neurotransmitters serotonin, norepinephrine, and dopamine seem to reduce symptoms of depression.
(B) ECT is never used prior to attempting psychotherapy or medication.
(C) Succinylcholine completely immobilizes the patient's body.
(D) ECT generally works faster than antidepressants.
(E) One ECT treatment is often sufficient to reduce symptoms of depression significantly.

This is a SPECIFIC question (subtype: Inference). The answer to an inference question must be directly supported by evidence from the text. As always, be sure to pay particular attention to the precise words used in the answer choices and how they relate to the information presented in the passage.

For answer choice (**A**), the third paragraph specifically states that ECT *affects* these particular neurotransmitters. However, no information is provided to suggest how these neurotransmitters are affected. Since the passage does not indicate an increase in these neurotransmitters, this cannot be the best answer. [Out of Scope]

The third paragraph states that *ECT is generally used in severely depressed patients for whom psychotherapy and medication prove ineffective*. This does not mean that ECT is *never* used before these other therapies. Answer choice (**B**) is too extreme to be the correct answer for this inference question. [One Word Wrong]

According to the third paragraph, succinylcholine renders muscle contractions *virtually non-existent*, rather than *completely* nonexistent. Moreover, the passage states that a patient's hand or foot may rhythmically move during ECT. Thus the patient's body is not *completely* immobilized. Eliminate answer choice (**C**). [One Word Wrong]

The paragraph also states that ECT may be used *when there is an imminent risk of suicide, since antidepressants often take several weeks to work effectively*. The conjunction *since* indicates that the length of time ECT takes to work is being contrasted with that of antidepressants. That is, it is implied that ECT works faster than antidepressants, at least in general. Answer choice (**D**) is correct. We see that this choice can be justified directly from proof sentences from the passage.

The final sentence of the third paragraph states that *repeated applications* of ECT affect several neurotransmitters. However, we are told nothing about how many treatments are needed to achieve results of any kind. Answer choice (**E**) is incorrect. [Out of Scope]

> If a passage is silent about a particular point, you should not infer it or assume it from the passage.

5. According to the passage, which of the following statements is true?

(A) Most severely depressed individuals have suicidal thoughts.
(B) The general public was unaware of the bodily harm caused by unmodified ECT.
(C) Research into the side effects of ECT has only recently begun.
(D) ECT does not benefit individuals with anxiety disorders.
(E) Severe depression can have symptoms unrelated to emotional mood.

When you encounter a Specific question that has no key words in the question stem, you must use key words in the choices and apply the process of elimination.

This is a difficult SPECIFIC question (subtype: Lookup) that does not indicate a particular part of the passage in the question stem. Thus, you have to use key words from the answer choices, look up proof sentences, and eliminate choices one by one. Use your Skeletal sketch to quickly and accurately locate the important information in the passage, and then eliminate each answer choice as soon as you prove that it is not cited in the passage as true.

Answer choice (A) includes the key words *severely depressed* and *suicidal,* which lead us to the third paragraph of the passage. This paragraph indicates that ECT is considered as a treatment option *when there is an imminent risk of suicide.* However, nothing in the passage indicates the percentage (or number) of severely depressed individuals who have suicidal thoughts. The use of the word *Most* is unjustified. Answer choice (A) can be eliminated. [One Word Wrong]

Answer choice (B) includes the key words *bodily harm* and *unmodified ECT,* which lead us to the second paragraph (which gives examples of the *bodily harm* caused by ECT in some cases). This paragraph describes ways in which the public was aware of the bodily harm caused by unmodified ECT. This knowledge influenced the general public's strongly negative conception of the procedure. Answer choice (B) is incorrect. [Direct Contradiction]

In answer choice (C), the key words *only recently* prompt us to look for time references. The second sentence of the final paragraph cites *decades-old studies* of ECT. Thus, research has not recently begun. Answer choice (C) should be ruled out. [Direct Contradiction]

The first paragraph states that *ECT is extremely effective against severe depression, some acute psychotic states, and mania.* This does NOT necessarily mean that ECT is ineffective for *anxiety disorders.* With an "according to the passage" question, the correct answer must be provable by the passage text. Answer choice (D) is not shown by the passage to be true. [Out of Scope]

The final sentence of the passage states that a *memory malfunction* is a possible side effect of *severe depression.* A memory malfunction is clearly unrelated to emotional mood. Answer choice (E) is correct.

Chapter 7
of
READING COMPREHENSION

PASSAGES &
PROBLEM SETS

Problem Set

The following problem set consists of reading passages followed by a series of questions on each passage. Use the following guidelines as you complete this problem set:

1. Before you read each passage, identify whether it is long or short.

2. Preview the first question before reading, but do not look at any of the subsequent questions prior to reading the passage, since you will not be able to do this on the GMAT.

3. As you read the passage, apply the 7 principles of active, efficient reading. Create a Headline List (for short passages) or a Skeletal Sketch (for long passages). Then, use your Headline List or Skeletal Sketch to assist you in answering all the questions that accompany the passage.

4. Before answering each question, identify it as either a General question or a Specific question. Use the 7 strategies for Reading Comprehension to assist you in answering the questions.

5. On the GMAT, you will typically see three questions on short passages and four questions on long passages. However, in this problem set, you will see five questions associated with each passage. As such, use the following modified timing guidelines:

    For short passages: Spend approximately two to three minutes reading and creating your Headline List. Spend approximately 60 seconds answering General questions and between 60 to 90 seconds answering Specific questions. Do not spend more than nine minutes in total reading, writing, and answering all the questions on a short passage. (Keep in mind that on the real GMAT, when you only see three questions on a typical short passage, you should finish in approximately six minutes.)

    For long passages: Spend approximately three to four minutes reading and creating your Skeletal Sketch. Spend approximately 60 seconds answering General questions and between 60 to 90 seconds answering Specific questions. Do not spend more than nine minutes in total reading, writing, and answering all the questions on a long passage. (Keep in mind that on the real GMAT, when you only see four questions on a typical long passage, you should finish in approximately eight minutes.)

Passage A: Japanese Swords

Historians have long recognized the Japanese sword as one of the finest cutting weapons ever created. But to consider the sword that is synonymous with the samurai as merely a weapon is to ignore what makes it so special. The Japanese sword has always been considered a splendid weapon and even a spiritual entity. The traditional Japanese saying "The sword is the soul of the samurai" not only reflects the sword's importance to its wielder but also is indicative of its importance to its creator, the master smith.

Master smiths may not have been considered artists in the classical sense, but every one of them took great care in how he created a sword, and no sword was created in exactly the same way. The forging process of the blade itself took hundreds of hours as two types of steel were heated, hammered and folded together many times. This created a blade consisting of thousands of very thin layers that had an extremely sharp and durable cutting edge; at the same time, the blade was flexible and therefore less likely to break. It was common, though optional, for a master smith to place a physical signature on a blade; in addition, every master smith had a "structural signature" due to his own secret forging process. Each master smith brought a high level of devotion, skill, and attention to detail to the sword-making process, and the sword itself was a reflection of his personal honor and ability. This effort made each blade as unique as the samurai who wielded it; today the Japanese sword is recognized as much for its artistic merit as for its historical significance.

1. **The primary purpose of the passage is to**

(A) challenge the observation that the Japanese sword is highly admired by historians

(B) introduce new information about the forging of Japanese swords

(C) identify how the Japanese sword is now perceived as much for its artistic qualities as its military ones

(D) argue that Japanese sword makers were as much artists as they were smiths

(E) explain the value attributed to the Japanese sword

2. **Each of the following is mentioned in the passage EXCEPT**

(A) Every Japanese sword has a unique structure that can be traced back to a special forging process.
(B) Master smiths kept their forging techniques secret.
(C) The Japanese sword was considered by some to have a spiritual quality.
(D) Master smiths are now considered artists by most major historians.
(E) The Japanese sword is considered both a work of art and a historical artifact.

3. **The author is most likely to agree with which of the following observations?**

(A) The Japanese sword is the most important handheld weapon in history.
(B) The skill of the samurai is what made the Japanese sword so special.
(C) If a sword had a physical signature, other swords could be attributed to that sword's creator.
(D) Master smiths were more concerned about the artistic merit of their blades than about the blades' practical qualities.
(E) The Japanese sword has more historical importance than artistic importance.

4. **Which of the following can be inferred about the term "structural signature" in this passage?**

(A) It indicates the inscription that the smith places on the blade during the forging process.
(B) It implies the particular characteristics of a blade created by a smith's unique forging process.
(C) It suggests that each blade can be traced back to a known master smith.
(D) It reflects the soul of the samurai who wielded it.
(E) It refers to the actual curved shape of the blade.

5. **One function of the second paragraph of the passage is to**

(A) present an explanation for a change in perception
(B) determine the historical significance of Japanese swords
(C) explain why each Japanese sword is unique
(D) compare Japanese master smiths to classical artists
(E) review the complete process of making a Japanese sword

Passage B: Television's Invention

In the early years of television, Vladimir Zworykin was, at least in the public sphere, recognized as its inventor. His loudest champion was his boss, David Sarnoff, then president of RCA and a man that we regard even today as "the father of television." Current historians agree, however, that Philo Farnsworth, a self-educated prodigy who was the first to transmit live images, was television's true inventor.

In his own time, Farnsworth's contributions went largely unnoticed, in large part because he was excluded from the process of introducing the invention to a national audience. Sarnoff put televisions into living rooms, and Sarnoff was responsible for a dominant paradigm of the television industry that continues to be relevant today: advertisers pay for the programming so that they can have a receptive audience for their products. Sarnoff had already utilized this construct to develop the radio industry, and it had, within ten years, become ubiquitous. Farnsworth thought the television should be used as an educational tool, but he had little understanding of the business world, and was never able to implement his ideas.

Perhaps one can argue that Sarnoff simply adapted the business model for radio and television from the newspaper industry, replacing the revenue from subscriptions and purchases of individual newspapers with that of selling the television sets themselves, but Sarnoff promoted himself as nothing less than a visionary. Some television critics argue that the construct Sarnoff implemented has played a negative role in determining the content of the programs themselves, while others contend that it merely created a democratic platform from which the audience can determine the types of programming it wants.

1. **The primary purpose of the passage is to**

(A) correct public misconception about Farnsworth's role in developing early television programs
(B) debate the influence of television on popular culture
(C) challenge the current public perception of Vladimir Zworykin
(D) chronicle the events that led up to the invention of the television
(E) describe Sarnoff's influence on the public perception of television's inception, and debate the impact of Sarnoff's paradigm

2. **It can be inferred from the third paragraph of the passage that**

(A) television shows produced by David Sarnoff and Vladimir Zworykin tended to earn negative reviews
(B) educational programs cannot draw as large an audience as sports programs
(C) a number of critics feel that Sarnoff's initial decision to earn television revenue through advertising has had a positive or neutral impact on content
(D) educational programs that are aired in prime time, the hours during which the greatest number of viewers are watching television, are less likely to earn a profit than those that are aired during the daytime hours
(E) in matters of programming, the audience's preferences should be more influential than those of the advertisers

3. **Which of the following best illustrates the relationship between the second and third paragraphs?**

(A) The second paragraph dissects the evolution of a contemporary controversy; the third paragraph presents differing viewpoints on that controversy.
(B) The second paragraph explores the antithetical intentions of two men involved in the infancy of an industry; the third paragraph details the eventual deterioration of that industry.
(C) The second paragraph presents differing views of a historical event; the third paragraph represents the author's personal opinion about that event.
(D) The second paragraph provides details that are necessary to support the author's opinion, which is presented in the third paragraph.
(E) The second paragraph presents divergent visions about the possible uses of a technological device; the third paragraph initiates a debate about the ramifications of one of those perspectives.

4. **According to the passage, the television industry, at its inception, earned revenue from**

(A) advertising only
(B) advertising and the sale of television sets
(C) advertising and subscriptions
(D) subscriptions and the sale of television sets
(E) advertising, subscriptions, and the sale of television sets

5. **The passage suggests that Farnsworth might have earned greater public notoriety for his invention if**

(A) Vladimir Zworykin had been less vocal about his own contributions to the television
(B) Farnsworth had been able to develop and air his own educational programs
(C) Farnsworth had involved Sarnoff in his plans to develop, manufacture, or distribute the television
(D) Sarnoff had involved Farnsworth in his plans to develop, manufacture, or distribute the television
(E) Farnsworth had a better understanding of the type of programming the audience wanted to watch most

Passage C: Life on Mars

Because of the proximity and likeness of Mars to Earth, scientists have long speculated about the possibility of life on Mars. As early as the mid-17th century, astronomers observed polar ice caps on Mars, and by the mid-19th century, scientists discovered other similarities to Earth, including the length of day and axial tilt. But in 1965, photos taken by the Mariner 4 probe revealed a Mars without rivers, oceans or signs of life. And in the 1990s, it was discovered that Mars, unlike Earth, no longer possessed a substantial global magnetic field, allowing celestial radiation to reach the planet's surface and solar wind to eliminate much of Mars's atmosphere over the course of several billion years.

More recent probes have focused on whether there was once water on Mars. Some scientists believe that this question is definitively answered by the presence of certain geological landforms. Others posit that different explanations, such as wind erosion or carbon dioxide oceans, may be responsible for these formations. Mars rovers Opportunity and Spirit, which have been exploring the surface of Mars since 2004, have both discovered geological evidence of past water activity. These findings substantially bolster claims that there was once life on Mars.

1. **The author's stance on the possibility of life on Mars can best be described as**

(A) optimistic
(B) disinterested
(C) skeptical
(D) simplistic
(E) cynical

2. **The passage is primarily concerned with which of the following?**

(A) disproving a widely accepted theory
(B) initiating a debate about the possibility of life on Mars
(C) presenting evidence in support of a controversial claim
(D) describing the various discoveries made concerning the possibility of life on Mars
(E) detailing the findings of the Mars rovers Opportunity and Spirit

*Manhattan*GMAT*Prep
the new standard

3. **Each of the following discoveries is mentioned in the passage EXCEPT**

(A) Wind erosion and carbon dioxide oceans are responsible for certain geological landforms on Mars.
(B) Mars does not have a substantial global magnetic field.
(C) Mars does not currently have water activity.
(D) The length of day on Mars is similar to that on Earth.
(E) The axial tilt of Mars is similar to that of Earth.

4. **In the first paragraph, the author most likely mentions the discovery of polar ice caps to suggest that**

(A) until recently Mars' polar ice caps were thought to consist largely of carbon dioxide
(B) Martian polar ice caps are made almost entirely of water ice
(C) Mars has many similarities to Earth, including the existence of polar ice caps
(D) Mars has only a small fraction of the carbon dioxide found on Earth and Venus
(E) conditions on the planet Mars were once very different than they are at present

5. **Each of the following can be inferred from the passage EXCEPT**

(A) The presence of certain geological landforms is not definitive proof that there was once life on Mars.
(B) It is likely that there were few significant discoveries related to the possibility of life on Mars prior to the mid-17th century.
(C) The absence of a substantial global magnetic field on Mars suggests that it would be difficult to sustain life on Mars.
(D) The presence of water activity on Mars is related to the possibility of life on Mars.
(E) The claim that there was once water on Mars has only limited and indirect support from recent discoveries.

Passage D: Fossils

In archaeology, as in the physical sciences, new discoveries frequently undermine accepted findings and give rise to new theories. This trend can be seen in the reaction to the recent discovery of a set of 3.3-million-year-old fossils in Ethiopia, the remains of the earliest well-preserved child ever found. The fossilized child was estimated to be about 3 years old at death, female, and a member of the Australopithecus afarensis species. The afarensis species, a major human ancestor, lived in Africa from earlier than 3.7 million to 3 million years ago. "Her completeness, antiquity and age at death make this find of unprecedented importance in the history of paleo-anthropology," said Zeresenay Alemseged, a noted paleo-anthropologist. Other scientists said that the discovery could reconfigure conceptions about the lives and capacities of these early humans.

Prior to this discovery, it had been thought that the afarensis species had abandoned the arboreal habitat of their ape cousins. However, while the lower limbs of this fossil supported findings that afarensis walked upright, its gorilla-like arms and shoulders suggested that it retained the ability to swing through trees. This has initiated a reexamination of many accepted theories of early human development. Also, the presence of a hyoid bone, a rarely preserved bone in the larynx that supports muscles of the throat, has had a tremendous impact on theories about the origins of speech. The fossil bone is primitive and more similar to that of apes than to that of humans, but it is the first hyoid found in such an early human-related species.

1. **The organization of the passage could best be described as**

(A) discussing a controversial scientific discovery
(B) contrasting previous theories of development with current findings
(C) illustrating a contention with a specific example
(D) arguing for the importance of a particular field of study
(E) refuting a popular misconception

2. **The passage quotes Zeresenay Alemseged in order to**

(A) provide evidence to qualify the main idea of the first paragraph
(B) question the claims of other scientists
(C) provide evidence to support the linguistic abilities of the afarensis species
(D) provide evidence that supports the significance of the find
(E) provide a subjective opinion that is refuted in the second paragraph

3. **Each of the following is cited as a factor in the importance of the discovery of the fossils EXCEPT**

(A) the fact that the remains were those of a child
(B) the age of the fossils
(C) the location of the discovery
(D) the species of the fossils
(E) the intact nature of the fossils

4. **It can be inferred from the passage's description of the discovered fossil hyoid bone that**

(A) Australopithecus afarensis were capable of speech
(B) the discovered hyoid bone is less primitive than the hyoid bone of apes
(C) the hyoid bone is necessary for speech
(D) the discovery of the hyoid bone necessitated the reexamination of prior theories
(E) the hyoid bone was the most important fossil found at the site

5. **According to the passage, the impact of the discovery of the hyoid bone in the field of archaeology could best be compared to which one of the following examples in another field?**

(A) The discovery and analysis of cosmic rays lend support to a widely accepted theory of the origin of the universe.
(B) The original manuscript of a deceased 19th century author confirms ideas of the development of an important work of literature.
(C) The continued prosperity of a state-run economy stirs debate in the discipline of macroeconomics.
(D) Newly revealed journal entries by a prominent Civil War era politician lead to a questioning of certain accepted historical interpretations about the conflict.
(E) Research into the mapping of the human genome gives rise to nascent applications of individually tailored medicines.

Passage E: Polygamy

Polygamy in Africa has been a popular topic for social research over the past four decades; it has been analyzed by many distinguished minds and in various well-publicized works. In 1961, when Remi Clignet published his book "Many Wives, Many Powers," he was not alone in sharing the view that in Africa co-wives may be perceived as direct and indirect sources of increased income and prestige.

By the 1970s, such arguments had become crystallized and popular. Many other African scholars who wrote on the subject became the new champions of this philosophy. For example, in 1983, John Mbiti proclaimed that polygamy is an accepted and respectable institution serving many useful social purposes. Similarly, G.K. Nukunya, in his paper "Polygamy as a Symbol of Status," reiterated Mbiti's idea that a plurality of wives is a sign of affluence and power in the African society.

However, the colonial missionary voice provided consistent opposition to polygamy by viewing the practice as unethical and destructive of family life. While they propagated this view with the authority of the Bible, they were convinced that Africans had to be coerced into partaking in the vision of monogamy understood by the Western culture. The missionary viewpoint even included, in some instances, dictating immediate divorce in the case of newly converted men who had already contracted polygamous marriages. Unfortunately, both the missionary voice and the scholarly voice did not consider the views of African women on the matter important. Although there was some awareness that women regarded polygamy as both a curse and a blessing, the distanced, albeit scientific, perspective of an outside observer predominated both on the pulpit and in scholarly writings.

Contemporary research in the social sciences has begun to focus on the protagonist's voice in the study of culture, recognizing that the views and experiences of those who take part in a given reality ought to receive close examination. This privileging of the protagonist seems appropriate, particularly given that women in Africa have often used literary productions to comment on marriage, family and gender relations.

1. **Which of the following best describes the main purpose of the passage above?**

(A) to discuss scholarly works that view polygamy as a sign of prestige, respect, and affluence in the African society

(B) to trace the origins of the missionary opposition to African polygamy

(C) to argue for imposing restrictions on polygamy in the African society

(D) to explore the reasons for women's acceptance of polygamy

(E) to discuss multiple perspectives on African polygamy and contrast them with contemporary research

2. **The third paragraph of the passage plays which of the following roles?**

(A) discusses the rationale for viewing polygamy as an indication of prestige and affluence in the African society

(B) supports the author's view that polygamy is unethical and destructive of family life

(C) contrasts the views of the colonial missionary with the position of the most recent contemporary research

(D) describes the views on polygamy held by the colonial missionary and indicates a flaw in this vision

(E) demonstrates that the colonial missionary was ignorant of the scholarly research on monogamy

3. **The passage provides each of the following, EXCEPT**

(A) the year of publication of Remi Clignet's book "Many Wives, Many Powers"

(B) the year in which John Mbiti made a claim that polygamy is an accepted institution

(C) examples of African women's literary productions devoted to family relations

(D) reasons for missionary opposition to polygamy

(E) current research perspectives on polygamy

4. **According to the passage, the colonial missionary and the early scholarly research shared which of the following traits in their views on polygamy?**

(A) both considered polygamy a sign of social status and success

(B) neither accounted for the views of local women

(C) both attempted to limit the prevalence of polygamy

(D) both pointed out polygamy's destructive effects on family life

(E) both exhibited a somewhat negative attitude towards polygamy

5. **Which of the following statements can most properly be inferred from the passage?**

(A) Nukunya's paper "Polygamy as a Symbol of Status" was not written in 1981.

(B) John Mbiti adjusted his initial view on polygamy, recognizing that the experiences of African women should receive closer attention.

(C) Remi Clignet's book "Many Wives, Many Powers" was the first well-known scholarly work to proclaim that polygamy can be viewed as a symbol or prestige and wealth.

(D) Under the influence of the missionary opposition, polygamy was proclaimed illegal in Africa as a practice "unethical and destructive of family life."

(E) A large proportion of the scholars writing on polygamy in the 1970s and 1980s were of African descent.

Passage F: Sweet Spot

Though most tennis players generally strive to strike the ball on the racket's vibration node, more commonly known as the "sweet spot," many players are unaware of the existence of a second, lesser-known location on the racket face, the center of percussion, that will also greatly diminish the strain on a player's arm when the ball is struck.

In order to understand the physics of this second sweet spot, it is helpful to consider what would happen to a tennis racket in the moments after impact with the ball if the player's hand were to vanish at the moment of impact. The impact of the ball would cause the racket to bounce backwards, experiencing a translational motion away from the ball. The tendency of this motion would be to jerk all parts of the racket, including the end of its handle, backward, or away from the ball. Unless the ball happened to hit the racket precisely at the racket's center of mass, the racket would additionally experience a rotational motion around its center of mass—much as a penny that has been struck near its edge will start to spin. Whenever the ball hits the racket face, the effect of this rotational motion will be to jerk the end of the handle forward, towards the ball. Depending on where the ball strikes the racket face, one or the other of these motions will predominate.

However, there is one point of impact, known as the center of percussion, which causes neither motion to predominate; if a ball were to strike this point, the impact would not impart any motion to the end of the handle. The reason for this lack of motion is that the force on the upper part of the hand would be equal and opposite to the force on the lower part of the hand, resulting in no net force on the tennis players' hand or forearm. The center of percussion constitutes a second sweet spot because a tennis player's wrist typically is placed next to the end of the racket's handle. When the player strikes the ball at the center of percussion, her wrist is jerked neither forward nor backward, and she experiences a relatively smooth, comfortable tennis stroke.

The manner in which a tennis player can detect the center of percussion on a given tennis racket follows from the nature of this second sweet spot. The center of percussion can be located via simple trial and error by holding the end of a tennis racket between your finger and thumb and throwing a ball onto the strings. If the handle jumps out of your hand, then the ball has missed the center of percussion.

1. **What is the primary message the author is trying to convey?**

(A) a proposal for an improvement to the design of tennis rackets
(B) an examination of the differences between the two types of sweet spot
(C) a definition of the translational and rotational forces acting on a tennis racket
(D) a description of the ideal area in which to strike every ball
(E) an explanation of a lesser-known area on a tennis racket that dampens unwanted vibration

2. **According to the passage, all of the following are true of the forces acting upon a tennis racket striking a ball EXCEPT**

(A) The only way to eliminate the jolt that accompanies most strokes is to hit the ball on the center of percussion.
(B) The impact of the ball striking the racket can strain a tennis player's arm.
(C) There are at least two different forces acting upon the racket.
(D) The end of the handle of the racket will jerk forward after striking the ball unless the ball strikes the racket's center of mass.
(E) The racket will rebound after it strikes the ball.

3. **What is the primary function served by paragraph two in the context of the entire passage?**

(A) to establish the main idea of the passage
(B) to provide an explanation of the mechanics of the phenomenon discussed in the passage
(C) to introduce a counterargument that elucidates the main idea of the passage
(D) to provide an example of the primary subject described in the passage
(E) to explain why the main idea of the passage would be useful for tennis players

4. **The author mentions "a penny that has been struck near its edge" in order to**

(A) show how the center of mass causes the racket to spin
(B) argue that a penny spins in the exact way that a tennis racket spins
(C) explain how translational motion works
(D) provide an illustration of a concept
(E) demonstrate that pennies and tennis rackets do not spin in the same way

5. **Which of the following can be inferred from the passage?**

(A) If a player holds the tennis racket anywhere other than the end of the handle, the player will experience a jolting sensation.
(B) The primary sweet spot is more effective at damping vibration than the secondary sweet spot.
(C) Striking a tennis ball at a spot other than the center of percussion can result in a jarring feeling.
(D) Striking a tennis ball repeatedly at spots other than a sweet spot leads to "tennis elbow."
(E) If a player lets go of the racket at the moment of impact, the simultaneous forward and backward impetus causes the racket to drop straight to the ground.

Passage G: Chaos Theory

Around 1960, mathematician Edward Lorenz found unexpected behavior in apparently simple equations representing atmospheric air flows. Whenever he reran his model with the same inputs, different outputs resulted—although the model lacked any random elements. Lorenz realized that tiny rounding errors in his analog computer mushroomed over time, leading to erratic results. His findings marked a seminal moment in the development of chaos theory, which, despite its name, has little to do with randomness.

To understand how unpredictability can arise from deterministic equations, which do not involve chance outcomes, consider the non-chaotic system of two poppy seeds placed in a round bowl. As the seeds roll to the bowl's center, a position known as a point attractor, the distance between the seeds shrinks. If, instead, the bowl is flipped over, two seeds placed on top will roll away from each other. Such a system, while still not technically chaotic, enlarges initial differences in position.

Chaotic systems, such as a machine mixing bread dough, are characterized by both attraction and repulsion. As the dough is stretched, folded and pressed back together, any poppy seeds sprinkled in are intermixed seemingly at random. But this randomness is illusory. In fact, the poppy seeds are captured by "strange attractors," staggeringly complex pathways whose tangles appear accidental but are in fact determined by the system's fundamental equations.

During the dough-kneading process, two poppy seeds positioned next to each other eventually go their separate ways. Any early divergence or measurement error is repeatedly amplified by the mixing until the position of any seed becomes effectively unpredictable. It is this "sensitive dependence on initial conditions" and not true randomness that generates unpredictability in chaotic systems, of which one example may be the Earth's weather. According to the popular interpretation of the "Butterfly Effect," a butterfly flapping its wings causes hurricanes. A better understanding is that the butterfly causes uncertainty about the precise state of the air. This microscopic uncertainty grows until it encompasses even hurricanes. Few meteorologists believe that we will ever be able to predict rain or shine for a particular day years in the future.

1. **The main purpose of this passage is to**

(A) explain complicated aspects of certain physical systems
(B) trace the historical development of a scientific theory
(C) distinguish a mathematical pattern from its opposite
(D) describe the spread of a technical model from one field of study to others
(E) contrast possible causes of weather phenomena

2. **In the example discussed in the passage, what is true about poppy seeds in bread dough, once the dough has been thoroughly mixed?**

(A) They have been individually stretched and folded over, like miniature versions of the entire dough.
(B) They are scattered in random clumps throughout the dough.
(C) They are accidentally caught in tangled objects called strange attractors.
(D) They are bound to regularly dispersed patterns of point attractors.
(E) They are in positions dictated by the underlying equations that govern the mixing process.

3. **According to the passage, the rounding errors in Lorenz's model**

(A) indicated that the model was programmed in a fundamentally faulty way
(B) were deliberately included to represent tiny fluctuations in atmospheric air currents
(C) were imperceptibly small at first, but tended to grow
(D) were at least partially expected, given the complexity of the actual atmosphere
(E) shrank to insignificant levels during each trial of the model

4. **The passage mentions each of the following as an example or potential example of a chaotic or non-chaotic system EXCEPT**

(A) a dough-mixing machine
(B) atmospheric weather patterns
(C) poppy seeds placed on top of an upside-down bowl
(D) poppy seeds placed in a right-side up bowl
(E) fluctuating butterfly flight patterns

5. **It can be inferred from the passage that which of the following pairs of items would most likely follow typical pathways within a chaotic system?**

(A) two particles ejected in random directions from the same decaying atomic nucleus
(B) two stickers affixed to a balloon that expands and contracts over and over again
(C) two avalanches sliding down opposite sides of the same mountain
(D) two baseballs placed into an active tumble dryer
(E) two coins flipped into a large bowl

Answers to Passage A: Japanese Swords

Historians have long recognized the Japanese sword as one of the finest cutting weapons ever created. But to consider the sword that is synonymous with the samurai as merely a weapon is to ignore what makes it so special. The Japanese sword has always been considered a splendid weapon and even a spiritual entity. The traditional Japanese saying "The sword is the soul of the samurai" not only reflects the sword's importance to its wielder but also is indicative of its importance to its creator, the master smith.

Master smiths may not have been considered artists in the classical sense, but every one of them took great care in how he created a sword, and no sword was created in exactly the same way. The forging process of the blade itself took hundreds of hours as two types of steel were heated, hammered and folded together many times. This created a blade consisting of thousands of very thin layers that had an extremely sharp and durable cutting edge; at the same time, the blade was flexible and therefore less likely to break. It was common, though optional, for a master smith to place a physical signature on a blade; in addition, every master smith had a "structural signature" due to his own secret forging process. Each master smith brought a high level of devotion, skill, and attention to detail to the sword-making process, and the sword itself was a reflection of his personal honor and ability. This effort made each blade as unique as the samurai who wielded it; today the Japanese sword is recognized as much for its artistic merit as for its historical significance.

This is a short passage (35 lines or fewer on page). Here is a model Headline List:

1) H: J sword = 1 of best cutting weapons, but even more spec   ← Point
   —Spiritual
   —Impt to wielder + creator (mr smith)

2) Mr smiths -- great care with swords, all unique
   —(Forging)
   —(Phys + struct sig)

1. The primary purpose of the passage is to

(A) challenge the observation that the Japanese sword is highly admired by historians
(B) introduce new information about the forging of Japanese swords
(C) identify how the Japanese sword is now perceived as much for its artistic qualities as its military ones
(D) argue that Japanese sword makers were as much artists as they were smiths
(E) explain the value attributed to the Japanese sword

To identify the primary purpose of the passage, you should examine the passage as a whole. Avoid answer choices that address only limited sections of the passage. The Point of the passage (*the Japanese sword is not just a fine weapon but something even more special*) is clearly established in the first two sentences; the purpose of the passage is to explain and support that Point.

(A) The passage does not call into question the admiration that historians have for the Japanese sword.

(B) The second paragraph of the passage discusses forging techniques, but none of the information is presented as new. Moreover, these forging techniques are not the focus of the passage.

(C) The artistic merit of the Japanese sword is identified in the last sentence of the second paragraph, but this is not the primary focus of the passage. Much of the passage discusses the sword's physical properties, not the perception of its artistic qualities.

(D) The passage describes some of the similarities between a master smith and an artist; however, these similarities are presented in the second paragraph, and not throughout the passage. Much of the passage describes the Japanese sword's physical properties and reasons for its importance.

(E) CORRECT. The passage as a whole describes the immense value of the Japanese sword to both the samurai (the sword's owner) and the smith (its maker). The saying *The sword is the soul of the samurai* is referenced in the first paragraph to indicate this importance. The second paragraph proceeds to detail the tremendous effort that is put into each sword, reflecting the importance of each one.

2. Each of the following is mentioned in the passage EXCEPT

(A) Every Japanese sword has a unique structure that can be traced back to a special forging process.
(B) Master smiths kept their forging techniques secret.
(C) The Japanese sword was considered by some to have a spiritual quality.
(D) Master smiths are now considered artists by most major historians.
(E) The Japanese sword is considered both a work of art and a historical artifact.

For an "EXCEPT" question (almost always a Specific question), you should use the process of elimination to identify and cross out those details mentioned in the passage.

(A) In the passage this *unique signature* is referred to as a *structural signature*.

(B) The second paragraph contains the following phrases: *every master smith...due to his own secret forging process.*

(C) The first paragraph indicates that *the Japanese sword has always been considered a splendid weapon and even a spiritual entity.*

(D) CORRECT. The time and effort master smiths devote to making a sword is discussed, and the passage does indicate that the Japanese sword is considered a unique work of art and of artistic merit. However, the passage does not state that most major historians consider master smiths themselves to be artists. *Major* historians are not referenced in the passage. Also, the passage states in the second paragraph that *Master smiths may not have been considered artists in the classical sense.*

(E) In the last sentence, the passage indicates that *the Japanese sword is recognized as much for its artistic merit as for its historical significance.*

3. The author is most likely to agree with which of the following observations?

(A) The Japanese sword is the most important handheld weapon in history.
(B) The skill of the samurai is what made the Japanese sword so special.
(C) If a sword had a physical signature, other swords could be attributed to that sword's creator.
(D) Master smiths were more concerned about the artistic merit of their blades than about the blades' practical qualities.
(E) The Japanese sword has more historical importance than artistic importance.

When looking for statements with which the author could agree, be sure to avoid extreme words and positions that go beyond the author's statements in the passage. This question requires attention to both the general Point of the passage and specific details throughout.

(A) The opening sentence says that *historians have long recognized the Japanese sword as one of the finest cutting weapons ever created*; however, there is no indication that the Japanese sword is the most important handheld weapon in history. There could be many others (e.g. handguns).

(B) This passage does not discuss the skill of the samurai warrior.

(C) CORRECT. In the second paragraph it says every master smith had a *structural signature* due to his own secret forging process. Therefore, if a physical signature is present on a blade, that blade's structural signature could then be associated with a master smith, whose *master* status implies the creation of numerous swords.

(D) The passage mentions that *the sword itself was a reflection of his [the creator's] personal honor and ability*; however, there is no claim that master smiths emphasized their swords' artistic merit at the expense of practical qualities.

(E) The passage acknowledges that the Japanese sword is important both historically and artistically, but the author does not stress the sword's historical importance over its artistry.

4. **Which of the following can be inferred about the term "structural signature" in this passage?**

   (A) It indicates the inscription that the smith places on the blade during the forging process.
   (B) It implies the particular characteristics of a blade created by a smith's unique forging process.
   (C) It suggests that each blade can be traced back to a known master smith.
   (D) It reflects the soul of the samurai who wielded it.
   (E) It refers to the actual curved shape of the blade.

In the second paragraph, the author states that *every master smith had a "structural signature" due to his own secret forging process*. The word *signature* implies the uniqueness of the smith's process. Be careful not to infer any additional information, particularly when the question refers to a specific sentence or phrase.

(A) In the passage, such an inscription is referred to as a *physical signature*, not a *structural signature*.

(B) CORRECT. Note that the proof sentence indicates that each smith had his own process, and so the *"structural signature"* was unique to each smith (not necessarily to each individual blade).

(C) This statement seems reasonable. However, the passage does not say whether all master smiths are currently *known*. Certain swords with a structural signature may be of unknown origin.

(D) The first paragraph mentions the saying *The sword is the soul of the samurai*, but we are not told that the structural signature was the aspect of the sword reflecting the soul of the samurai who wielded it. The second paragraph explains that the sword was a *reflection of his [i.e., the smith's] personal honor and ability* and that each sword was *as unique as the samurai who wielded it*. Neither of these statements, however, justifies the claim that the *structural signature* itself *reflects the soul of the samurai who wielded it*.

(E) The passage does not discuss the shape of the Japanese blade.

5. **One function of the second paragraph of the passage is to**

   (A) present an explanation for a change in perception
   (B) determine the historical significance of Japanese swords
   (C) explain why each Japanese sword is unique
   (D) compare Japanese master smiths to classical artists
   (E) review the complete process of making a Japanese sword

Manhattan **GMAT** Prep
the new standard

To determine the function(s) of any paragraph, pay attention to the emphasized content of the paragraph, in particular any reiterated points, and to the relationship the paragraph has to other paragraphs. In this case, the second paragraph extends the idea introduced in the first paragraph that the Japanese sword is *special* and a *unique work of art.*

(A) The second paragraph mentions that Japanese swords are now appreciated more for their artistic merit, but no explanation is provided.

(B) The term *historical significance* closes the second paragraph, but no information is given in the second paragraph to explain or outline that significance.

(C) **CORRECT.** In several places, the second paragraph underscores the uniqueness of individual Japanese swords. The first sentence mentions that *no sword was created in exactly the same way.* Later in the second paragraph, it is mentioned that *every master smith had a "structural signature"*; finally, the last sentence indicates that *this effort made each blade as unique as the samurai who wielded it.*

(D) The passage explains that master smiths were not considered artists in the classical sense, and then goes on to point out the painstaking creation of each sword. This implicitly draws a parallel between the creation of the sword and classical artistry. However, the passage does not actually describe or discuss classical artists, nor does it set forth criteria for classical artists. There is no actual comparison to classical artists, despite the mention of *artistic merit.* This answer choice goes too far beyond the passage; thus, it is incorrect.

(E) Elements of the forging process are discussed, but the whole or *complete* process of making a Japanese sword, such as making the handle, polishing the blade, etc. is not discussed in the paragraph.

Answers to Passage B: Television's Invention

In the early years of television, Vladimir Zworykin was, at least in the public sphere, recognized as its inventor. His loudest champion was his boss, David Sarnoff, then president of RCA and a man that we regard even today as "the father of television." Current historians agree, however, that Philo Farnsworth, a self-educated prodigy who was the first to transmit live images, was television's true inventor.

In his own time, Farnsworth's contributions went largely unnoticed, in large part because he was excluded from the process of introducing the invention to a national audience. Sarnoff put televisions into living rooms, and Sarnoff was responsible for a dominant paradigm of the television industry that continues to be relevant today: advertisers pay for the programming so that they can have a receptive audience for their products. Sarnoff had already utilized this construct to develop the radio industry, and it had, within ten years, become ubiquitous. Farnsworth thought the television should be used as an educational tool, but he had little understanding of the business world, and was never able to implement his ideas.

Perhaps one can argue that Sarnoff simply adapted the business model for radio and television from the newspaper industry, replacing the revenue from subscriptions and purchases of individual newspapers with that of selling the television sets themselves, but Sarnoff promoted himself as nothing less than a visionary. Some television critics argue that the construct Sarnoff implemented has played a negative role in determining the content of the programs themselves, while others contend that it merely created a democratic platform from which the audience can determine the types of programming it wants.

This is a short passage (35 lines or fewer on page). Here is a model Headline List:

---

1) Early TV yrs, Z seen = TV invntr
   —champ by RCA pres Sarn (father of TV!)
   BUT now hist agree: F = TRUE invntr

2) F excluded fr proc intro TV to pub
   —S intro'd, resp for domin paradigm: advrs pay   ← Point
   —F: TV shd be educ

3) Maybe S just adapted newsppr model
   —bad for content vs. democ platform?

1. The primary purpose of the passage is to

(A) correct public misconception about Farnsworth's role in developing early television programs
(B) debate the influence of television on popular culture
(C) challenge the current public perception of Vladimir Zworykin
(D) chronicle the events that led up to the invention of the television
(E) describe Sarnoff's influence on the public perception of television's inception, and debate the impact of Sarnoff's paradigm

The answer to a primary purpose question should incorporate elements of the entire passage. Avoid answer choices that address limited sections of the passage. The Point that the author wants to convey (in the second paragraph) is that Sarnoff was responsible for introducing television to the public and creating a dominant paradigm. This is foreshadowed in the first paragraph, in which Sarnoff is called *the father of television*. The purpose of the passage should reflect the Point.

(A) Farnsworth's influence on the development of the television itself is only mentioned in paragraphs one and two, but not in the last paragraph. Farnsworth's role in developing programs is never mentioned, nor is the correction of a public misconception the focus of the passage.

(B) The impact of television is not discussed until the final paragraph. Although the last paragraph debates whether or not Sarnoff's influence was a positive one, it does not address the influence of television on popular culture.

(C) Vladimir Zworykin is only mentioned briefly in the first paragraph, so he is clearly not the primary subject of the passage. Furthermore, even though we know the initial public perception, we know nothing about the current public perception of Zworykin.

(D) The passage discusses events that occurred after the invention; there is no mention of the events that led up to the invention of the television.

(E) CORRECT. This answer includes the main elements of all three paragraphs; it functions as a good summary of the entire passage.

2. It can be inferred from the third paragraph of the passage that

(A) television shows produced by David Sarnoff and Vladimir Zworykin tended to earn negative reviews
(B) educational programs cannot draw as large an audience as sports programs
(C) a number of critics feel that Sarnoff's initial decision to earn television revenue through advertising has had a positive or neutral impact on content
(D) educational programs that are aired in prime time, the hours during which the greatest number of viewers are watching television, are less likely to earn a profit than those that are aired during the daytime hours
(E) in matters of programming, the audience's preferences should be more influential than those of the advertisers

The third paragraph states that some critics viewed Sarnoff's paradigm negatively and others thought it embodied a democratic concept. The correct answer must follow from those statements.

(A) We have been given no information about the television programs Sarnoff and Zworykin produced; in fact, we have not been told that they produced television shows. The paragraph is about the advertising revenue construct Sarnoff implemented, not about the television shows he produced.

(B) It is implied that ratings for educational programs are, in general, not strong, but that does not mean that any one particular educational program cannot have higher ratings than one particular sports program. Beware of answer choices that contain absolutes such as *cannot*.

(C) CORRECT. We are told that *some television critics argue that Sarnoff's paradigm has played a negative role in determining the content*. Since the word is *some*, it must be true that others either feel it has played a positive role, or a neutral role.

(D) The passage does not differentiate programming based on what time television shows air, nor does it mention profitability.

(E) The word "should" implies a moral judgment, and the answer is therefore out of the scope of the passage. Furthermore, the third paragraph does not indicate a belief as to who should properly influence programming choices.

3. **Which of the following best illustrates the relationship between the second and third paragraphs?**

(A) The second paragraph dissects the evolution of a contemporary controversy; the third paragraph presents differing viewpoints on that controversy.
(B) The second paragraph explores the antithetical intentions of two men involved in the infancy of an industry; the third paragraph details the eventual deterioration of that industry.
(C) The second paragraph presents differing views of a historical event; the third paragraph represents the author's personal opinion about that event.
(D) The second paragraph provides details that are necessary to support the author's opinion, which is presented in the third paragraph.
(E) The second paragraph presents divergent visions about the possible uses of a technological device; the third paragraph initiates a debate about the ramifications of one of those perspectives.

The structure question requires you both to grasp the main idea of each paragraph and to consider how they are related to each other. The second paragraph presents the differences between Sarnoff and Farnsworth's perspectives. The third paragraph presents differing points of view on the impact that Sarnoff's paradigm has had. The correct answer will incorporate those points.

(A) It is unclear what *contemporary controversy* the second paragraph explores. The second paragraph is about the differences between Sarnoff and Farnsworth--these differences do not represent a controversy nor are they contemporary. The third paragraph presents differing points of view about the impact that Sarnoff's paradigm has had. The differing points of view are not related to the material in the second paragraph.

(B) Though they had different visions of what television could be, Farnsworth and Sarnoff did not have visions that were *antithetical*, or the opposites of each other. Additionally, there is no evidence presented in the third paragraph that alludes to the deterioration of the television industry.

(C) In the second paragraph, we are given differing visions of what could be, not differing opinions of something that has already happened. The author provides opposing viewpoints, but refrains from presenting his or her own opinion on the debate.

(D) The author provides opposing viewpoints, but refrains from presenting his or her own opinion on the debate.

(E) CORRECT. The second paragraph expresses two different visions of how to use the television; the third paragraph explores the impact of the adoption of Sarnoff's vision.

> **4. According to the passage, the television industry, at its inception, earned revenue from**
>
> (A) advertising only
> (B) advertising and the sale of television sets
> (C) advertising and subscriptions
> (D) subscriptions and the sale of television sets
> (E) advertising, subscriptions, and the sale of television sets

In order to trick you on a specific question such as this, the GMAT will offer incomplete answers that incorporate language from throughout the passage but do not directly bear on the question at hand. Two sections in the passage discuss ways in which the television industry brought in revenue. The second paragraph states that *advertisers pay for the programming so that they can have a receptive audience for their products.* The third paragraph states that the television industry benefited by *replacing the revenue from subscriptions and purchases of individual newspapers with that of selling the television sets themselves.*

(A) This answer choice does not account for the revenue generated from selling television sets.

(B) CORRECT. Advertising and the sale of television sets are the two ways mentioned through which the industry could generate revenue.

(C) Subscriptions are mentioned as a method for newspapers to earn revenue; the last paragraph clearly states that television replaced this revenue with that earned by selling the sets themselves.

(D) This choice does not mention advertising revenue; moreover, it incorrectly mentions subscription revenue.

(E) This answer choice incorrectly mentions subscription revenue.

5. **The passage suggests that Farnsworth might have earned greater public notoriety for his invention if**

(A) Vladimir Zworykin had been less vocal about his own contributions to the television
(B) Farnsworth had been able to develop and air his own educational programs
(C) Farnsworth had involved Sarnoff in his plans to develop, manufacture, or distribute the television
(D) Sarnoff had involved Farnsworth in his plans to develop, manufacture, or distribute the television
(E) Farnsworth had a better understanding of the type of programming the audience wanted to watch most

Farnsworth's notoriety, or lack thereof, is discussed at the beginning of the second paragraph: *In his own time, Farnsworth's contributions went largely unnoticed, in large part because he was excluded from the process of introducing the invention to a national audience.* Thus, the passage clearly suggests that if he had been included in that process of introducing the invention, his contributions would have been noticed more widely.

(A) There is no mention made of Zworykin being vocal about his own contributions. Furthermore, the passage hints at no connection between Zworykin's self-promotion and Farnsworth's lack of notoriety.

(B) Though we have been told that Farnsworth wanted to use television as an educational tool, we have not been told that he wanted to develop television shows himself. Additionally, it is debatable whether the development of educational television programs would have significantly contributed to Farnsworth's public notoriety.

(C) The passage states that Farnsworth was the one who was excluded, not the one who prevented others from getting involved.

(D) CORRECT. The passage states that Farnsworth's contributions went unnoticed partly because he was excluded from the process of introducing the invention to the audience. If he had been involved in the development, manufacture, or distribution, he would have been involved in the introduction process, and it logically follows that this could have led to greater notoriety.

(E) The passage does not connect Farnsworth's lack of notoriety with a lack of understanding about the television audience, nor does it state in any way Farnsworth's opinions about the audience.

Answers to Passage C: Life on Mars

Because of the proximity and likeness of Mars to Earth, scientists have long speculated about the possibility of life on Mars. As early as the mid-17th century, astronomers observed polar ice caps on Mars, and by the mid-19th century, scientists discovered other similarities to Earth, including the length of day and axial tilt. But in 1965, photos taken by the Mariner 4 probe revealed a Mars without rivers, oceans or signs of life. And in the 1990s, it was discovered that Mars, unlike Earth, no longer possessed a substantial global magnetic field, allowing celestial radiation to reach the planet's surface and solar wind to eliminate much of Mars's atmosphere over the course of several billion years.

More recent probes have focused on whether there was once water on Mars. Some scientists believe that this question is definitively answered by the presence of certain geological landforms. Others posit that different explanations, such as wind erosion or carbon dioxide oceans, may be responsible for these formations. Mars rovers Opportunity and Spirit, which have been exploring the surface of Mars since 2004, have both discovered geological evidence of past water activity. These findings substantially bolster claims that there was once life on Mars.

This is a short passage (35 lines or fewer on page). Here is a model Headline List:

1) S: Mars close, simil to Earth → poss life on M!
   —Sims (polar ice, day, tilt)
   —Diffs (no water, no more mag field)

2) Rec focus: was there water?
   —Evid: yes/no, now <u>more</u> support → <u>was</u> life on M   ← Point

1. **The author's stance on the possibility of life on Mars can best be described as**

(A) optimistic
(B) disinterested
(C) skeptical
(D) simplistic
(E) cynical

This passage is concerned with the possibility of life on Mars. It details the various discoveries that have been made since the mid-17th century. The passage can best be described as factual and unbiased. When considering a tone question such as this, look for instances in which the author's opinion is revealed. You should also remember to be wary of extreme words in the answer choices.

(A) The author is neither optimistic nor pessimistic about the possibility of life on Mars.

(B) CORRECT. Note that the primary meaning of *disinterested* is "impartial" or "neutral," which accurately describes the tone of the argument.

(C) There is no indication that the author of the passage is skeptical. The passage simply puts forth facts and does not offer an opinion one way or the other.

(D) The author considers several different factors in the determination of life on Mars. The author's stance could not appropriately be described as simplistic.

(E) Again, the author is objective in tone and could not accurately be characterized as cynical.

2. **The passage is primarily concerned with which of the following?**

(A) disproving a widely accepted theory
(B) initiating a debate about the possibility of life on Mars
(C) presenting evidence in support of a controversial claim
(D) describing the various discoveries made concerning the possibility of life on Mars
(E) detailing the findings of the Mars rovers Opportunity and Spirit

This passage is primarily concerned with the possibility of life on Mars. The two paragraphs discuss various discoveries that have been made over the past several centuries. The passage concludes that recent findings substantiate claims that there was once life on Mars. However, scientists are still not certain. In determining the purpose or main idea of the passage, it is important to avoid extreme words and to be able to defend every word.

(A) This passage does not set out to *disprove* the theory that there is life on Mars. It is also too extreme to suggest that this is a *widely accepted* theory.

(B) This answer choice is tempting because it is relatively neutral. However, the passage does not seek to *initiate* a debate; it is more concerned with documenting findings that pertain to life on Mars. In other words, the passage presents the findings that frame a debate, not initiating the debate itself.

the new standard

(C) The passage presents evidence in support of and against the possibility of life on Mars. It is too limited to suggest that the passage is primarily concerned with presenting evidence *in support of* life of Mars.

(D) CORRECT. This answer choice avoids extreme words and best summarizes the purpose of the passage.

(E) This answer choice is too specific. The passage does mention the Mars rovers Opportunity and Spirit, but it is inaccurate to suggest that the passage is primarily concerned with these two rovers.

3. **Each of the following discoveries is mentioned in the passage EXCEPT**

    (A) Wind erosion and carbon dioxide oceans are responsible for certain geological landforms on Mars.
    (B) Mars does not have a substantial global magnetic field.
    (C) Mars does not currently have water activity.
    (D) The length of day on Mars is similar to that on Earth.
    (E) The axial tilt of Mars is similar to that of Earth.

To address this Specific question, point out specific evidence in the text to defend your answer choice. The passage discusses several discoveries; to answer this question, find which of the answer choices is NOT a discovery specifically mentioned in the passage.

(A) CORRECT. The passage does make mention of wind erosion and carbon dioxide oceans, but the author states that these are other possible explanations for certain geological landforms on Mars. Wind erosion and carbon dioxide oceans are *possible* causes of the geological landforms rather than discoveries.

(B) At the end of the first paragraph, the passage states that *in the 1990s, it was discovered that Mars, unlike Earth, no longer possessed a substantial global magnetic field.*

(C) The Mariner 4 probe revealed in 1965 that there are no rivers or oceans (water activity) on Mars in the third sentence of the first paragraph.

(D) Certain similarities of Mars to Earth were discovered in the mid-19th century, including the length of day in the second sentence of the first paragraph.

(E) Certain similarities of Mars to Earth were discovered in the mid-19th century, including the axial tilt of Mars being similar to that of the Earth in the second sentence of the first paragraph.

4. **In the first paragraph, the author most likely mentions the discovery of polar ice caps to suggest that**

(A) until recently Mars' polar ice caps were thought to consist largely of carbon dioxide
(B) Martian polar ice caps are made almost entirely of water ice
(C) Mars has many similarities to Earth, including the existence of polar ice caps
(D) Mars has only a small fraction of the carbon dioxide found on Earth and Venus
(E) conditions on the planet Mars were once very different than they are at present

This is a Specific question that refers back to the second sentence in the first paragraph. The best approach is to reread this sentence and determine, using surrounding sentences, what the author's purpose is in mentioning Mars' polar ice caps. If we read the second part of the sentence, *by the mid-19th century, scientists discovered other similarities to Earth, including the length of day and axial tilt*, we notice that polar ice caps are introduced as an example of the similarity of Mars to Earth.

(A) The passage does not mention the content of the polar ice caps, just that they were observed.

(B) Again, we do not know, from the passage, the composition of Mars' polar ice caps.

(C) CORRECT. As stated above, polar ice caps are introduced as one of several similarities of Mars to Earth.

(D) The passage does not indicate the carbon dioxide content or Mars or Earth. It also does not mention Venus.

(E) While we know from the rest of the passage that conditions on Mars were probably different than they are now, the author does not mention polar ice caps in order to indicate this.

5. **Each of the following can be inferred from the passage EXCEPT**

(A) The presence of certain geological landforms is not definitive proof that there was once life on Mars.
(B) It is likely that there were few significant discoveries related to the possibility of life on Mars prior to the mid-17th century.
(C) The absence of a substantial global magnetic field on Mars suggests that it would be difficult to sustain life on Mars.
(D) The presence of water activity on Mars is related to the possibility of life on Mars.
(E) The claim that there was once water on Mars has only limited and indirect support from recent discoveries.

Manhattan **GMAT** Prep
the new standard

A question that asks for an inference from the passage is a specific question; it is helpful to find evidence for any inference in the text. Make sure each inference can be defended by going back to the text, and does not go far beyond the language in the passage.

(A) In the second paragraph, the author states that while the presence of geological landforms may indicate the presence of water, it is also possible that these landforms were caused by wind erosion or carbon dioxide oceans.

(B) The first discoveries mentioned were as early as the mid-17th century. Therefore, it is reasonable to conclude that it is likely that there were not many significant discoveries before this time. Notice that this inference avoids extreme words: It does not say that there were no discoveries, just that it is not *likely* that many preceded this period.

(C) In the second paragraph, the absence of a substantial global magnetic field is presented as evidence of the lack of life on Mars. Again, note that this answer choice avoids extreme words by using the word *suggests*.

(D) The first sentence in the second paragraph states that *more recent probes have focused on whether or not there was once water on Mars.* Given this purpose, it is clear that the existence of water is important in order to establish whether or not there was life on Mars.

(E) CORRECT. According to the second paragraph, the Mars rovers Opportunity and Spirit *have both discovered geological evidence of past water activity.* This is both significant (as made clear by the subsequent sentence that *these findings substantially bolster claims...*) and direct evidence supporting the claim that there was once water on Mars. Thus, the passage contradicts the statement that this claim is supported by only limited and indirect evidence.

Answers to Passage D: Fossils

In archaeology, as in the physical sciences, new discoveries frequently undermine accepted findings and give rise to new theories. This trend can be seen in the reaction to the recent discovery of a set of 3.3-million-year-old fossils in Ethiopia, the remains of the earliest well-preserved child ever found. The fossilized child was estimated to be about 3 years old at death, female, and a member of the Australopithecus afarensis species. The afarensis species, a major human ancestor, lived in Africa from earlier than 3.7 million to 3 million years ago. "Her completeness, antiquity and age at death make this find of unprecedented importance in the history of paleo-anthropology," said Zeresenay Alemseged, a noted paleo-anthropologist. Other scientists said that the discovery could reconfigure conceptions about the lives and capacities of these early humans.

Prior to this discovery, it had been thought that the afarensis species had abandoned the arboreal habitat of their ape cousins. However, while the lower limbs of this fossil supported findings that afarensis walked upright, its gorilla-like arms and shoulders suggested that it retained the ability to swing through trees. This has initiated a reexamination of many accepted theories of early human development. Also, the presence of a hyoid bone, a rarely preserved bone in the larynx that supports muscles of the throat, has had a tremendous impact on theories about the origins of speech. The fossil bone is primitive and more similar to that of apes than to that of humans, but it is the first hyoid found in such an early human-related species.

This is a short passage (35 lines or fewer on page). Here is a model Headline List:

1) In arch, new disc → undermine old, lead to new thries   ← Point
   —Child fossils of af. species in Eth

2) Before: thought af. abandnd arb hab of apes
   BUT this disc → reexam old thry of hum dev
   Also hy bone → chg thries ab speech

1. The organization of the passage could best be described as

    (A) discussing a controversial scientific discovery
    (B) contrasting previous theories of human development with current theories
    (C) illustrating a general contention with a specific example
    (D) arguing for the importance of a particular field of study
    (E) refuting a popular misconception

When assessing a passage's organization, consider the main idea of each paragraph. This passage begins by noting that *new discoveries frequently undermine accepted findings and give rise to new theories* in archaeology. It supports this statement by relating the impact of one discovery in the field. Thus, the best answer will reference both the contention and the use of the example.

(A) This choice omits the phenomenon that the discovery is meant to illustrate, which is that discoveries often give rise to new theories. Also, there is nothing controversial about the described discovery.

(B) The passage does not focus on the contrast between previous theories of human development and current theories. Rather, it discusses a singular discovery that affects previous theories. The passage would need to outline both previous and current theories of development and then contrast them. Instead, the passage focuses on how one example illustrates a way in which the field of archeology evolves.

(C) CORRECT. The passage makes a general claim and uses a specific example to support that claim, just as this choice states.

(D) One might feel that the evolution of theories of human development is a worthwhile object of contemplation, but the <u>passage</u> does not argue for the importance of archaeology as a field of study. This answer choice misstates the organization of the passage.

(E) The passage does not indicate how widely held earlier theories of human development were. Indeed, they are too esoteric to be properly classified as a *popular misconception*. Also, the passage is organized around the example of a single discovery and its importance. The language employed in the passage does not warrant describing the passage as a refutation of past theories.

2. The passage quotes Zeresenay Alemseged in order to

    (A) provide evidence to qualify the main idea of the first paragraph
    (B) question the claims of other scientists
    (C) provide evidence to support the linguistic abilities of the afarensis species
    (D) provide evidence that supports the significance of the find
    (E) provide a subjective opinion that is refuted in the second paragraph

This quotation in the first paragraph highlights the importance of the discovery and is followed by another similar reference. The quotation is used to emphasize the exceptional importance of this find; the correct answer for this Inference question will reflect this emphasis.

(A) The main idea of the first paragraph is that a new finding can call accepted archaeological theories into question. The rest of the paragraph provides an example of this phenomenon. However, the quotation emphasizes the importance of the discovery itself. Moreover, even if you take a broad interpretation of the quotation's role, the quotation does not qualify or limit the main idea of the first paragraph.

(B) The passage does not discuss claims of other scientists. Thus, this answer choice is incorrect.

(C) The discussion of the linguistic ability of the afarensis species is in the second paragraph and is unrelated to this quotation.

(D) CORRECT. The point of this paragraph is to illustrate that archeology is like a physical science in that important factual discoveries lead to theoretical changes. The quotation provides evidence that this discovery is in fact a significant one.

(E) The quotation is offered as evidence of the importance of the discovery, and is not refuted at any point in the passage.

3. **Each of the following is cited as a factor in the importance of the discovery of the fossils EXCEPT**

(A) the fact that the remains were those of a child
(B) the age of the fossils
(C) the location of the discovery
(D) the species of the fossils
(E) the intact nature of the fossils

With a question of this sort, instead of looking for the correct answer, it is often easier to eliminate incorrect answer choices based on the information provided in the passage.

(A) The fifth sentence of the first paragraph cites a quotation from a noted paleo-anthropologist that the find of the child fossils was of unprecedented importance due to the child's *age at death*. Therefore, the fact that the remains were those of a child was of substantial significance.

(B) The *antiquity* (a synonym for *age*) of the fossils is mentioned in the first paragraph as a reason why the fossils were an important discovery.

(C) CORRECT. The location of the fossil discovery is mentioned in the first paragraph of the passage. However, the location is not provided as a reason why the fossils are significant.

(D) The fossils are described in the second paragraph of the passage as impacting *accepted theories of early human development*. The fossils are also shown to be important to the development of speech. These implications would not be applicable if the fossils were not of a species of human ancestor (e.g. the fossils of an ancient elephant). Also, there were specific preconceptions of the afarensis species that were called into question by the discovery of the fossils. Thus, the species of the fossils is of particular significance to the discovery.

(E) The fifth sentence of the first paragraph notes that the find was important due its *completeness*. The intact nature of the fossils is another way of saying that the fossils are complete.

the new standard

4. **It can be inferred from the passage's description of the discovered fossil hyoid bone that**

   (A) Australopithecus afarensis were capable of speech
   (B) the discovered hyoid bone is less primitive than the hyoid bone of apes
   (C) the hyoid bone is necessary for speech
   (D) the discovery of the hyoid bone necessitated the reexamination of prior theories
   (E) the hyoid bone was the most important fossil found at the site

The passage provides the following information about the discovered hyoid bone: it is the oldest ever found since the bone is rarely preserved and it *is primitive and more similar to those of apes than humans.* The passage also states the discovery will impact theories about speech. A good inference is a point that must follow <u>directly</u> from one of these statements.

(A) The passage gives no information about the linguistic capacities of Australopithecus afarensis. The passage does not give enough information to infer that they were capable of speech.

(B) The passage indicates that the discovered hyoid bone more closely resembles those of apes than humans. However, while the passage does generally relate to evolution, the discovered bone is not necessarily less primitive than that of an ape. It could be slightly different in an equally primitive way; not all differences in structure would make a bone more advanced.

(C) While it can be inferred that this bone has an effect on speech, the passage does not indicate that it is *necessary* for speech. It is possible that a modern species could be capable of speech without a hyoid bone.

(D) CORRECT. The passage states that the discovery of the hyoid bone *has had a tremendous impact on theories about the origins of speech.* The passage goes on to say that it is the first hyoid found in such an early human-related species, suggesting that the timeline of human verbal development would be changed by the discovery. Thus, it can be inferred that the discovery made the reexamination of prior theories necessary.

(E) The passage does not rank the importance of the fossils found; as a result, this choice is not necessarily correct. It is possible that other fossils were of equal or greater importance.

5. **According to the passage, the impact of the discovery of the hyoid bone in the field of archaeology could best be compared to which one of the following examples in another field?**

   (A) The discovery and analysis of cosmic rays lend support to a widely accepted theory of the origin of the universe.
   (B) The original manuscript of a deceased 19th century author confirms ideas of the development of an important work of literature.
   (C) The continued prosperity of a state-run economy stirs debate in the discipline of macroeconomics.
   (D) Newly revealed journal entries by a prominent Civil War era politician lead to a questioning of certain accepted historical interpretations about the conflict.
   (E) Research into the mapping of the human genome gives rise to nascent applications of individually tailored medicines.

When you are asked to choose which answer best parallels a part of a passage, be sure that you grasp the nature of the comparison on the passage side before considering the answer choices.

The passage indicates that the discovery of the hyoid bone *has had a tremendous impact on theories about the origins of speech.* The author also places this discovery in parallel to discoveries of other bones of this particular fossil, which have *initiated a reexamination of many accepted theories of early human development.*

These sentences indicate that the discovery of the hyoid bone has either expanded or called into question certain previously held ideas in the field. The correct answer will reflect this sort of impact in another field.

(A) This answer choice discusses the impact of the discovery and analysis of cosmic rays on the field of physics. However, in this example the discovery serves to support a widely accepted theory, as opposed to causing a reexamination of earlier ideas.

(B) This answer choice describes the original manuscript of an author that confirms ideas of the development of an important work of literature. However, in this answer choice the discovery serves to confirm earlier held ideas, as opposed to causing a reexamination of accepted ideas.

(C) This answer choice describes a current phenomenon, the continued success of a state-run economy, that stirs debate in the discipline of macroeconomics. This example is dissimilar from the discovery of the hyoid bone in a number of ways. First, the success of a state-run economy is a contemporary phenomenon rather than a discovery. Also, the provocation of debate is not analogous to a *reexamination of accepted theories,* as there is no indication that an accepted macroeconomic theory is applicable and being called into question. Last, the state-run economy in question could be the latest example in a long line of successful controlled economies, as opposed to being a discovery of any importance.

(D) CORRECT. This answer choice correctly describes a discovery that causes a reexamination of earlier ideas in another field. In this case, newly uncovered journal entries by a politician spur a re-evaluation of certain historical ideas regarding an important conflict.

(E) This answer choice describes scientific advances in the field of biology as giving rise to new applications. It does not discuss a discovery that calls accepted ideas into question.

Answers to Passage E: Polygamy

Polygamy in Africa has been a popular topic for social research over the past four decades; it has been analyzed by many distinguished minds and in various well-publicized works. In 1961, when Remi Clignet published his book "Many Wives, Many Powers," he was not alone in sharing the view that in Africa co-wives may be perceived as direct and indirect sources of increased income and prestige.

By the 1970s, such arguments had become crystallized and popular. Many other African scholars who wrote on the subject became the new champions of this philosophy. For example, in 1983, John Mbiti proclaimed that polygamy is an accepted and respectable institution serving many useful social purposes. Similarly, G.K. Nukunya, in his paper "Polygamy as a Symbol of Status," reiterated Mbiti's idea that a plurality of wives is a sign of affluence and power in the African society.

However, the colonial missionary voice provided consistent opposition to polygamy by viewing the practice as unethical and destructive of family life. While they propagated this view with the authority of the Bible, they were convinced that Africans had to be coerced into partaking in the vision of monogamy understood by the Western culture. The missionary viewpoint even included, in some instances, dictating immediate divorce in the case of newly converted men who had already contracted polygamous marriages. Unfortunately, both the missionary voice and the scholarly voice did not consider the views of African women on the matter important. Although there was some awareness that women regarded polygamy as both a curse and a blessing, the distanced, albeit scientific, perspective of an outside observer predominated both on the pulpit and in scholarly writings.

Contemporary research in the social sciences has begun to focus on the protagonist's voice in the study of culture, recognizing that the views and experiences of those who take part in a given reality ought to receive close examination. This privileging of the protagonist seems appropriate, particularly given that women in Africa have often used literary productions to comment on marriage, family and gender relations.

This is a long passage (more than 35 lines on page). Here is a model Skeletal Sketch:

---

1) <u>Past 4 decs: Polygamy in Afr = pop topic soc rsch</u>
   —'61 Clig: co-wives = income, prestige

2) By 70s others agree
   —Many other Afr scholars

3) BUT missnry opp polygamy
   —Unfortly — miss + scholars: view of Afr wmn NOT impt   ← Point (part)

4) Curr rsch: exps of protagonists (Afr wmn)   ← Point (part)

---

1. Which of the following best describes the main purpose of the passage above?

(A) to discuss scholarly works that view polygamy as a sign of prestige, respect, and affluence in the African society
(B) to trace the origins of the missionary opposition to African polygamy
(C) to argue for imposing restrictions on polygamy in the African society
(D) to explore the reasons for women's acceptance of polygamy
(E) to discuss multiple perspectives on African polygamy and contrast them with contemporary research

On questions asking about the main idea of the passage, be sure to avoid extreme answer choices and those answers that refer to only a part of the passage rather than the whole text. Typically, test writers will include several incorrect answers that will be factually true but will describe the purpose of just one paragraph. The Point of this passage is arguably split in at least two pieces. The author wants to convey not only that two views of polygamy in Africa (those of the early scholars and of the missionaries) were *unfortunately* limited, but also that current research is addressing this limitation by bringing in the perspectives of the women protagonists.

(A) Scholarly works that view polygamy as a sign of prestige and affluence are discussed only in the first two paragraphs of the passage. This answer is too narrow to capture the purpose of the entire text.

(B) While the third paragraph discusses the missionary opposition and traces its sources to the Bible, this analysis is not central to the entire passage and is thus too narrow to capture the scope of the entire text.

(C) While the text discusses multiple perspectives on polygamy, it does not argue in favor or against restricting polygamy.

(D) The passage provides no information about the reasons that women accept polygamy, other than mentioning that they view it as both *a curse and a blessing.*

(E) CORRECT. The entire passage is devoted to the discussion of multiple perspectives on polygamy. The first two paragraphs review scholarly works that view polygamy as a sign of prestige and respect, while the third paragraph offers an opposing view. Finally, the concluding paragraph contrasts both of these perspectives with contemporary research.

2. The third paragraph of the passage plays which of the following roles?

(A) discusses the rationale for viewing polygamy as an indication of prestige and affluence in the African society
(B) supports the author's view that polygamy is unethical and destructive of family life
(C) contrasts the views of the colonial missionary with the position of the most recent contemporary research
(D) describes the views on polygamy held by the colonial missionary and indicates a flaw in this vision
(E) demonstrates that the colonial missionary was ignorant of the scholarly research on monogamy

This question asks us to summarize the role of the third paragraph. On this type of question, it is helpful to reread the topic sentence of the paragraph at issue. The topic sentence is typically in the first or second sentence of the paragraph. Furthermore, look for the answer that effectively captures the entire paragraph and avoids making unjustified statements.

(A) These scholarly works are discussed in the first and second rather than the third paragraph.

(B) While the third paragraph discusses the views of the colonial missionary, nothing in the passage suggests that the author shares this vision.

(C) While the third paragraph presents the position of the colonial missionary, the most recent contemporary research is discussed only in the concluding paragraph of the passage.

(D) CORRECT. The second paragraph describes the position of the colonial missionary and indicates a flaw in this perspective. Note that the missionary's position is described in the opening sentence of the paragraph: *However, the colonial missionary voice provided consistent opposition to polygamy by viewing the practice as unethical and destructive of family life.* Furthermore, after discussing this position, the author goes on to identify a deficiency in this reasoning: *Unfortunately, both the missionary voice and the scholarly voice did not consider the views of African women on the matter important.*

(E) While the third paragraph discusses the perspective of the colonial missionary, nothing is mentioned in the passage about the attitude of the missionary towards scholarly research on monogamy.

3. The passage provides each of the following, EXCEPT

(A) the year of publication of Remi Clignet's book "Many Wives, Many Powers"
(B) the year in which John Mbiti made a claim that polygamy is an accepted institution
(C) examples of African women's literary productions devoted to family relations
(D) reasons for missionary opposition to polygamy
(E) current research perspectives on polygamy

On detail questions, you can facilitate your decision process by looking for signal words. Since this is an "EXCEPT" question, we can answer it by findings the statements that were mentioned in the passage and eliminating them from our consideration set. In this process, make sure to use proper nouns (such as Remi Clignet) and dates (such as 1983) as your signals. Since dates and capitalized nouns stand out in the text, they can speed up the process of verifying the answer choices. (Of course, be aware that a wrong answer choice might include words from the passage but fail to include the idea behind the words.)

(A) The second sentence of the opening paragraph states that Remi Clignet published his book "Many Wives, Many Powers" in 1961.

(B) According to the second sentence of the second paragraph, John Mbiti proclaimed that polygamy is an accepted and respectable institution in 1983.

(C) CORRECT. The concluding paragraph mentions that *women in Africa have often used literary productions to comment on marriage* but provides no specific examples of such works.

(D) According to the third paragraph of the passage, the colonial missionary opposed polygamy because it considered this practice *as unethical and destructive of family life.*

(E) The opening sentence of the last paragraph provides a detailed description of the position of contemporary research towards polygamy.

4. According to the passage, the colonial missionary and the early scholarly research shared which of the following traits in their views on polygamy?

(A) both considered polygamy a sign of social status and success
(B) neither accounted for the views of local women
(C) both attempted to limit the prevalence of polygamy
(D) both pointed out polygamy's destructive effects on family life
(E) both exhibited a somewhat negative attitude towards polygamy

To answer this detail question, we need to refer to paragraph three, which offers a comparison of the views of the colonial missionary and those of early scholars. Note that the correct answer will outline the trait that was shared by both groups, while incorrect answers will typically restate characteristics that were true of only one rather than both groups.

(A) While the early scholarly researchers indeed viewed polygamy as a sign of prestige, this perspective was not shared by the colonial missionary, who declared it *unethical and destructive of family life.*

(B) CORRECT. This statement is explicitly supported by the penultimate sentence of the third paragraph: *Unfortunately, both the missionary voice and the scholarly voice did not consider the views of African women on the matter important.*

(C) While the passage suggests that the colonial missionary may have attempted to limit the prevalence of polygamy by coercing Africans *into partaking in the vision of monogamy,* nothing in the passage suggests that the scholarly research shared this perspective.

(D) This view was characteristic of the colonial missionary, as discussed in the third paragraph, but not of the early scholarly research.

(E) According to the third paragraph, the colonial missionary certainly maintained a negative attitude towards polygamy, considering this practice *unethical and destructive of family life.* By contrast, early scholarly research considered this phenomenon *a sign of affluence and power.* Nothing in the passage suggests that the early scholars had a negative attitude towards polygamy.

5. **Which of the following statements can most properly be inferred from the passage?**

   (A) Nukunya's paper "Polygamy as a Symbol of Status" was not written in 1981.
   (B) John Mbiti adjusted his initial view on polygamy, recognizing that the experiences of African women should receive closer attention.
   (C) Remi Clignet's book "Many Wives, Many Powers" was the first well-known scholarly work to proclaim that polygamy can be viewed as a symbol or prestige and wealth.
   (D) Under the influence of the missionary opposition, polygamy was proclaimed illegal in Africa as a practice "unethical and destructive of family life."
   (E) A large proportion of the scholars writing on polygamy in the 1970s and 1980s were of African descent.

Since this is an inference question, we will be looking for an answer that can be inferred strictly based on the information given in the passage and without making any additional assumptions. Typically, the correct answer must be very closely connected to the actual text of the passage and directly supported by one or two sentences. Be sure to avoid inferences that may be seen as plausible but would require information not provided in the passage.

(A) CORRECT. The second paragraph states that Nukunya's work "Polygamy as a Symbol of Status" *reiterated Mbiti's idea that that plurality of wives is a sign of affluence and power....* Since Nukunya's work reiterated the views of Mbiti, "Polygamy as a Symbol of Status" must have been written <u>after</u> Mbiti expressed his perspective on polygamy. According to the text, it was not until 1983 that *John Mbiti proclaimed that polygamy is an accepted and respectable institution.* Therefore, Nukunya's "Polygamy as a Symbol of Status" must have been written after 1983; we can conclude that it was not written in 1981.

(B) While the text mentions that contemporary research acknowledges that the perspective of African women should receive closer attention, nothing in the passage suggests that Mbiti subsequently embraced this view and changed his initial stance.

(C) In the second sentence of the opening paragraph, the author states that *when Remi Clignet published his book "Many Wives, Many Powers," he was not alone in sharing the view…*, suggesting that at the time of publication, there were other scholarly works that viewed polygamy as a symbol or prestige and wealth. Therefore, Clignet's book was not the first to give this perspective.

(D) While the passage mentions that the colonial missionary opposed polygamy, viewing it as *unethical and destructive,* nothing in the passage suggests that polygamy was declared illegal in Africa.

(E) The passage provides no information regarding the background of the scholars who wrote about African polygamy. Moreover, even if this information were provided for the several examples of scholarly work mentioned in the passage, it would not be possible to make any conclusions about the scholars not mentioned in the passage.

Answers to Passage F: Sweet Spot

Though most tennis players generally strive to strike the ball on the racket's vibration node, more commonly known as the "sweet spot," many players are unaware of the existence of a second, lesser-known location on the racket face, the center of percussion, that will also greatly diminish the strain on a player's arm when the ball is struck.

In order to understand the physics of this second sweet spot, it is helpful to consider what would happen to a tennis racket in the moments after impact with the ball if the player's hand were to vanish at the moment of impact. The impact of the ball would cause the racket to bounce backwards, experiencing a translational motion away from the ball. The tendency of this motion would be to jerk all parts of the racket, including the end of its handle, backward, or away from the ball. Unless the ball happened to hit the racket precisely at the racket's center of mass, the racket would additionally experience a rotational motion around its center of mass—much as a penny that has been struck near its edge will start to spin. Whenever the ball hits the racket face, the effect of this rotational motion will be to jerk the end of the handle forward, towards the ball. Depending on where the ball strikes the racket face, one or the other of these motions will predominate.

However, there is one point of impact, known as the center of percussion, which causes neither motion to predominate; if a ball were to strike this point, the impact would not impart any motion to the end of the handle. The reason for this lack of motion is that the force on the upper part of the hand would be equal and opposite to the force on the lower part of the hand, resulting in no net force on the tennis players' hand or forearm. The center of percussion constitutes a second sweet spot because a tennis player's wrist typically is placed next to the end of the racket's handle. When the player strikes the ball at the center of percussion, her wrist is jerked neither forward nor backward, and she experiences a relatively smooth, comfortable tennis stroke.

The manner in which a tennis player can detect the center of percussion on a given tennis racket follows from the nature of this second sweet spot. The center of percussion can be located via simple trial and error by holding the end of a tennis racket between your finger and thumb and throwing a ball onto the strings. If the handle jumps out of your hand, then the ball has missed the center of percussion.

This is a long passage (more than 35 lines on page). Here is a model Skeletal Sketch:

---

1) Tennis plyrs try to hit ball on racket "sweet spot"
   <u>Many unaware: 2nd spot, CP, also dims arm strain</u>   ← Point

2) Assume no hand when ball hits, what happ?
   —Cd jerk handle back or fwd

3) If ball hits CP, no jerk—doesn't jerk wrist either

4) Can find CP w trial & error

---

1. What is the primary message the author is trying to convey?

(A) a proposal for an improvement to the design of tennis rackets
(B) an examination of the differences between the two types of sweet spot
(C) a definition of the translational and rotational forces acting on a tennis racket
(D) a description of the ideal area in which to strike every ball
(E) an explanation of a lesser-known area on a tennis racket that dampens unwanted vibration

The primary message the author is trying to convey is the Point. If you have identified the Point as the second half of the first paragraph, then you are ready to answer this question. The first paragraph introduces the idea that there are two sweet spots on the face of a tennis racket: one well-known spot and another *lesser-known* spot. The second and third paragraphs detail how the mechanism of the second sweet spot, the center of percussion, works. The fourth paragraph describes a way to find the center of percussion.

(A) Nothing in the passage suggests that the author is trying to propose an improvement to the design of tennis rackets. The second sweet spot exists independent of the design of the racket.

(B) The passage does mention both types of sweet spot in the first paragraph, but it does not focus on the differences between the two.

(C) Paragraph two explains the types of forces acting on the racket, but this topic is too narrow to be the primary message of the overall passage. The passage as a whole focuses on the sweet spots as opposed to the forces acting on the racket.

(D) While the passage does mention one benefit of hitting the ball on a sweet spot, it does not claim that this is the *ideal* area to hit *every* ball. There may be other areas that convey other benefits. The word *every* is too extreme.

(E) CORRECT. This matches our initial summary, above: the passage introduces the notion of a *second, lesser-known* sweet spot which can also *diminish the strain* when a player strikes the ball.

2. **According to the passage, all of the following are true of the forces acting upon a tennis racket striking a ball EXCEPT**

(A) The only way to eliminate the jolt that accompanies most strokes is to hit the ball on the center of percussion.
(B) The impact of the ball striking the racket can strain a tennis player's arm.
(C) There are at least two different forces acting upon the racket.
(D) The end of the handle of the racket will jerk forward after striking the ball unless the ball strikes the racket's center of mass.
(E) The racket will rebound after it strikes the ball.

"EXCEPT" questions require us to validate the answer choices. We must simply go through the choices one by one, labeling true answers with a T and the one false answer with an F.

(A) CORRECT. False. This choice contradicts information given in the first paragraph: the center of percussion is only one of two sweet spots which minimize vibration. The vibration node is the other sweet spot.

(B) True. The third sentence of the first paragraph introduces the concept that the impact can *strain* the player's arm.

(C) True. The second paragraph describes at least two different forces that act upon a tennis racket striking the ball: translational as described in the second and third sentences and rotational as described in the fourth and fifth sentences.

(D) True. The fourth sentence of the second paragraph states that *unless the ball happened to hit the racket precisely at the racket's center of mass, the racket would additionally experience a rotational motion.* The fifth sentence then reads *Whenever the ball hits the racket face, the effect of this rotational motion will be to jerk the end of the handle forward, towards the ball.*

(E) True. The second sentence of the second paragraph states that a racket will *bounce backward* after striking the ball; these words are synonyms for *rebound*.

3. **What is the primary function served by paragraph two in the context of the entire passage?**

(A) to establish the main idea of the passage
(B) to provide an explanation of the mechanics of the phenomenon discussed in the passage
(C) to introduce a counterargument that elucidates the main idea of the passage
(D) to provide an example of the primary subject described in the passage
(E) to explain why the main idea of the passage would be useful for tennis players

Paragraph two introduces and explains, in great detail, the forces that act on a racket when striking a ball. It specifically explains the means by which the *lesser-known* sweet spot, the center of percussion, functions.

(A) The main idea is established in the first paragraph: there is a second sweet spot that results in minimal vibration when a tennis racket strikes a ball. The second paragraph explains the forces that affect how this second sweet spot functions; it does not itself establish the main idea of the passage.

(B) CORRECT. This matches the description of the second paragraph above: it explains the mechanics of the second sweet spot in great detail.

(C) The second paragraph introduces the forces that act on a racket when striking a ball, and the concept of a center of percussion is explained. The first paragraph indicates the existence of the center of percussion; therefore, it would be incorrect to refer to the second paragraph as a counterargument.

(D) While the second paragraph does provide an example, this is not an example of the center of percussion, which is the primary subject described in the passage. The example helps to explain the forces behind the center of percussion, but is not itself an example of a center of percussion.

(E) The first and third paragraphs, not the second paragraph, make reference to why tennis players would want to know about the sweet spot: to minimize strain on the arm.

4. The author mentions "a penny that has been struck near its edge" in order to

(A) show how the center of mass causes the racket to spin
(B) argue that a penny spins in the exact way that a tennis racket spins
(C) explain how translational motion works
(D) provide an illustration of a concept
(E) demonstrate that pennies and tennis rackets do not spin in the same way

The full sentence expressed in the passage is *the racket would additionally experience a rotational motion around its center of mass—much as a penny that has been struck near its edge will start to spin.* In other words, the motion of the penny is an example that closely mimics the situation with the tennis racket. The correct answer should match this characterization.

(A) The center of mass does not cause the racket to spin; rather, a ball striking the racket causes it to spin.

(B) The author does not present the information about the penny as an argument; rather, it is an example. In addition, the author implies, via the words *much as,* that the penny and the racket spin in similar ways; this is not the same as saying that they spin in the *exact* same way.

(C) This sentence is about rotational motion, not translational motion.

(D) CORRECT. The example of the penny is an analogy for the rotational motion experienced by the tennis racket.

(E) The example is intended to demonstrate a situation in which tennis rackets and pennies do spin in similar ways.

the new standard

5. Which of the following can be inferred from the passage?

(A) If a player holds the tennis racket anywhere other than the end of the handle, the player will experience a jolting sensation.

(B) The primary sweet spot is more effective at damping vibration than the secondary sweet spot.

(C) Striking a tennis ball at a spot other than the center of percussion can result in a jarring feeling.

(D) Striking a tennis ball repeatedly at spots other than a sweet spot leads to "tennis elbow."

(E) If a player lets go of the racket at the moment of impact, the simultaneous forward and backward impetus causes the racket to drop straight to the ground.

Because the question applies to the whole passage, we must examine the answer choices first. It is useful to remember that when the GMAT asks us to *infer*, we need to base our inference only on information presented in the passage.

(A) The passage does explain that holding the racket at the end of the handle and hitting the ball at a particular spot results in a comfortable stroke that reduces the strain on a player's arm. It does not address, however, what would happen if the player grasped the racket at a different point. It is possible that grasping the racket at another point would simply result in a different center of percussion.

(B) The passage states that there is one commonly known sweet spot and a second, lesser-known sweet spot. However, the passage says nothing about the relative efficacy of these two sweet spots.

(C) CORRECT. We are told that playing tennis can result in strain on a player's arm. We are also told that striking the ball at the center of percussion leads to a *smooth, comfortable stroke* or one which does not cause the same kind of damage as a *regular* stroke. Striking the ball at a spot other than the center of percussion then, could lead to a jarring stroke, or one that could cause damage to a player's arm.

(D) The passage mentions nothing about "tennis elbow" or what behavior can result in this injury; it merely talks about *strain*. Be careful not to add additional information beyond what is presented in the passage.

(E) The second paragraph obliquely addresses a situation in which a tennis player lets go of the racket at the moment of impact. However, this question does not specify the point at which the tennis ball struck the racket. If the ball did not strike a sweet spot, the racket may have some translational or rotational force transferred from the ball.

Answers to Passage G: Chaos Theory

Around 1960, mathematician Edward Lorenz found unexpected behavior in apparently simple equations representing atmospheric air flows. Whenever he reran his model with the same inputs, different outputs resulted—although the model lacked any random elements. Lorenz realized that tiny rounding errors in his analog computer mushroomed over time, leading to erratic results. His findings marked a seminal moment in the development of chaos theory, which, despite its name, has little to do with randomness.

To understand how unpredictability can arise from deterministic equations, which do not involve chance outcomes, consider the non-chaotic system of two poppy seeds placed in a round bowl. As the seeds roll to the bowl's center, a position known as a point attractor, the distance between the seeds shrinks. If, instead, the bowl is flipped over, two seeds placed on top will roll away from each other. Such a system, while still not technically chaotic, enlarges initial differences in position.

Chaotic systems, such as a machine mixing bread dough, are characterized by both attraction and repulsion. As the dough is stretched, folded and pressed back together, any poppy seeds sprinkled in are intermixed seemingly at random. But this randomness is illusory. In fact, the poppy seeds are captured by "strange attractors," staggeringly complex pathways whose tangles appear accidental but are in fact determined by the system's fundamental equations.

During the dough-kneading process, two poppy seeds positioned next to each other eventually go their separate ways. Any early divergence or measurement error is repeatedly amplified by the mixing until the position of any seed becomes effectively unpredictable. It is this "sensitive dependence on initial conditions" and not true randomness that generates unpredictability in chaotic systems, of which one example may be the Earth's weather. According to the popular interpretation of the "Butterfly Effect," a butterfly flapping its wings causes hurricanes. A better understanding is that the butterfly causes uncertainty about the precise state of the air. This microscopic uncertainty grows until it encompasses even hurricanes. Few meteorologists believe that we will ever be able to predict rain or shine for a particular day years in the future.

This is a long passage (more than 35 lines on page). Here is a model Skeletal Sketch:

---

1) 1960 L: unexp behav in air flow eqs
   Reran model, diff results
   L: tiny rounding errors blew up → erratic results
   help dev <u>chaos thry</u>—<u>little to do with randomness</u>← Point

2) Unpredict can come fr determ eqs
   —non-chaotic: 2 poppy seeds in or on bowl

3) Dough mixing (chaos): seed movmnt <u>seems</u> random but is NOT

4) Seeds go sep ways → unpredict, not truly random
   —weather, butterfly eff

---

1. The main purpose of this passage is to

(A) explain complicated aspects of certain physical systems
(B) trace the historical development of a scientific theory
(C) distinguish a mathematical pattern from its opposite
(D) describe the spread of a technical model from one field of study to others
(E) contrast possible causes of weather phenomena

The passage's main purpose can be determined by identifying the Point of the passage and then examining the role of each paragraph. The first paragraph introduces chaos theory by describing a historical moment in its development. The Point comes at the end of the first paragraph, i.e., *chaos theory has little to do with randomness*. The next three paragraphs focus on further explaining this mystery, namely, the way in which *unpredictability can arise from deterministic equations, which do not involve chance outcomes*, as the first sentence of the second paragraph states. These paragraphs use analogies involving poppy seeds and bread dough to illustrate the explanations. Finally, as a minor addendum, the last paragraph mentions how this understanding of chaos theory might be applied to the weather, as a possible specific case of a chaotic system.

Taking all of these roles together, we see that the main purpose of the passage is to introduce chaos theory and explain how chaotic systems seem to be random but actually are governed by very complex equations.

(A) CORRECT. The *complicated aspects* are the characteristic features of chaotic systems, such as *sensitive dependence on initial conditions* and *staggeringly complex pathways*. The point of the passage is to explain such features.

(B) The first paragraph, as an introduction, describes a particular milestone in the historical development of chaos theory. However, the passage does not go on to describe other developments of this theory over time.

(C) Perhaps the behavior of chaotic systems could arguably be described as a *mathematical pattern*. However, the passage does not discuss any category of systems that are categorized clearly as the *opposite* of chaotic systems. Certain non-chaotic systems are described in the second paragraph, but it is not clear whether these systems would be the *opposite* of chaotic systems, or whether *random* systems would be the opposite.

(D) If chaos theory is the *technical model* mentioned in the answer choice, the passage never describes how that model spreads from one field of study to any other.

(E) Late in the fourth paragraph, the *"Butterfly Effect"* is mentioned as a popular explanation for at least some hurricanes. However, no other causes of weather phenomena are ever discussed.

2. **In the example discussed in the passage, what is true about poppy seeds in bread dough, once the dough has been thoroughly mixed?**

(A) They have been individually stretched and folded over, like miniature versions of the entire dough.
(B) They are scattered in random clumps throughout the dough.
(C) They are accidentally caught in tangled objects called strange attractors.
(D) They are bound to regularly dispersed patterns of point attractors.
(E) They are in positions dictated by the underlying equations that govern the mixing process.

The question asks about the poppy seeds in mixed bread dough. The third paragraph describes what happens to these poppy seeds: they *are intermixed seemingly at random.* But the positions of the seeds are not random, as the next sentences emphasize. Rather, the seeds *are captured by "strange attractors," staggeringly complex pathways whose tangles... are in fact determined by the system's fundamental equations.* Thus, the positions of the seeds are themselves *determined by the system's fundamental equations.*

(A) The passage mentions nothing about any stretching or folding of the poppy seeds themselves.

(B) The poppy seeds are scattered throughout the dough, but not in random clumps.

(C) The poppy seeds are caught in strange attractors, but there is nothing *accidental* about their capture. Moreover, the strange attractors described in the passage are not physical objects but rather mathematical pathways.

(D) Point attractors are not mentioned in relation to the dough-mixing process. Also, the poppy seeds, which have been *intermixed seemingly at random,* are not placed at regular intervals.

(E) CORRECT. The poppy seeds may seem to be scattered at random, but they follow the pathways of the strange attractors. These pathways, and thus the seeds' positions, have been *determined by the system's fundamental equations.*

*Manhattan*GMAT*Prep
the new standard

3. According to the passage, the rounding errors in Lorenz's model

(A) indicated that the model was programmed in a fundamentally faulty way
(B) were deliberately included to represent tiny fluctuations in atmospheric air currents
(C) were imperceptibly small at first, but tended to grow
(D) were at least partially expected, given the complexity of the actual atmosphere
(E) shrank to insignificant levels during each trial of the model

The question asks for specific details with the keywords *rounding errors* and *Lorenz's model.* The reference to Lorenz leads to the first paragraph, which contains the following sentence: *Lorenz realized that tiny rounding errors in his analog computer mushroomed over time, leading to erratic results.* In other words, the rounding errors started out small but became larger.

Because the question uses the words *according to the passage,* we should not try to draw any kind of inference. Rather, we should look for an answer that matches as closely as possible to the statements in the passage.

(A) Although these rounding errors are in fact *errors,* nothing in the passage indicates or implies that the model overall was built incorrectly.

(B) The errors were not deliberately included in the model. We know this from the passage's first sentence, which states that Lorenz found *unexpected behavior* in his model. It may be argued that the role of these errors is similar to the role of *tiny fluctuations in atmospheric air currents*— that is, they both introduce uncertainty that grows over time. However, this answer choice claims incorrectly that the errors were inserted on purpose.

(C) CORRECT. This answer choice corresponds very closely to the statement in the passage. Some synonyms have been used, but the meaning is the same: *were imperceptibly small at first* substitutes for *tiny,* and *tended to grow* substitutes for *mushroomed over time.*

(D) The passage indicates that the behavior of the model was unexpected. Nothing in the passage indicates that Lorenz expected the errors at all.

(E) The errors did not shrink but rather *mushroomed over time.*

4. The passage mentions each of the following as an example or potential example of a chaotic or non-chaotic system EXCEPT

(A) a dough-mixing machine
(B) atmospheric weather patterns
(C) poppy seeds placed on top of an upside-down bowl
(D) poppy seeds placed in a right-side-up bowl
(E) fluctuating butterfly flight patterns

The passage mentions several examples of systems, both chaotic and non-chaotic, to illustrate the special characteristics of chaos. This question is an exercise in finding the references to the four wrong answers quickly.

(A) A dough-mixing machine is first mentioned at the beginning of the third paragraph as an example of chaos in action: *Chaotic systems, such as a machine mixing bread dough…*

(B) Atmospheric weather patterns as a system to be studied are mentioned in both the first and the last paragraphs. In the last paragraph, the passage states that the Earth's weather may be an example of a chaotic system.

(C) Poppy seeds placed on an upside-down bowl are described in the second paragraph as an example of a non-chaotic system that creates divergence.

(D) Poppy seeds placed in a bowl that is right-side-up are described in the second paragraph as an example of a non-chaotic system that creates convergence.

(E) CORRECT. Butterfly flight patterns are nowhere mentioned as a system. According to the last paragraph, the "Butterfly Effect" is caused by the flapping of a single butterfly's wings to potentially affect atmospheric systems.

5. It can be inferred from the passage that which of the following pairs of items would most likely follow typical pathways within a chaotic system?

(A) two particles ejected in random directions from the same decaying atomic nucleus
(B) two stickers affixed to a balloon that expands and contracts over and over again
(C) two avalanches sliding down opposite sides of the same mountain
(D) two baseballs placed into an active tumble dryer
(E) two coins flipped into a large bowl

Stripped down to its essence, the question asks you to infer which of the five choices describes a system that is the most *chaotic*, according to the characteristics of chaos outlined in the passage. The most important proof sentence is at the beginning of the third paragraph: *Chaotic systems, such as a machine mixing bread dough, are characterized by both attraction and repulsion.* Thus, you should look for the system that is the most analogous to the dough-mixing machine. Moreover, the system should contain both attractive and repulsive elements: in other words, the two items embedded within the system should sometimes come near each other and then separate again.

At the beginning of the fourth paragraph, there is a "red herring" proof sentence: *During the dough-kneading process, two poppy seeds positioned next to each other eventually go their separate ways.* This sentence could lead you to think that the defining characteristic of chaotic systems is simply that two embedded items move away from each other. The question is asked in such a way as to focus your attention on the two items, so that you might then use this proof sentence alone and choose an incorrect answer.

(A) The two particles ejected from a nucleus do diverge, but they do not approach each other again. Moreover, there is no implication of any activity analogous to mixing bread dough.

(B) The stickers on the balloon separate and come together repeatedly. This behavior meets the criterion of *both attraction and repulsion*. However, there is no mixing, and as a result, the system cannot be said to be analogous to a machine mixing dough.

the new standard

(C) As in answer choice (A), the two items in question (avalanches) separate but never draw near each other again. Likewise, there is no mixing in the system.

(D) **CORRECT.** Two baseballs placed into an active tumble dryer are analogous to two poppy seeds placed in bread dough being mixed by a machine: parts of the system are separated, intermingled and brought back together again in perfectly regular, though complex, ways. The pathways of the two baseballs will diverge and converge repeatedly, as in any other chaotic system.

(E) The two coins flipped into a bowl is closely analogous to the example in the second paragraph of the passage of two poppy seeds placed in a bowl and allowed to fall; this system is presented as non-chaotic.

REAL GMAT PASSAGES & QUESTIONS

Now that you have completed your study of **READING COMPREHENSION**, it is time to test your skills on passages that have actually appeared on real GMAT exams over the past several years. These passages can be found in three books published by GMAC (Graduate Management Admission Council):

The Official Guide for GMAT Review, 12th Edition (pages 27–32 & 358–407),
The Official Guide for GMAT Verbal Review (pages 22–56), and
The Official Guide for GMAT Verbal Review, 2nd Edition (pages 22–59).

Note: The two editions of the Verbal Review book largely overlap. Use one OR the other.

Read each passage in the Reading Comprehension sections of the books above and answer all the questions associated with each passage using the following guidelines:

1. Before you read each passage, identify whether it is long or short. (Long passages are those with more than 35 lines on the page. Short passages are those with 35 lines or fewer.)

2. Preview the first question before reading, but do not look at any of the subsequent questions prior to reading the passage, since you will not be able to do this on the GMAT.

3. As you read the passage, apply the 7 principles of active, efficient reading. Create a Headline List (for short passages) or a Skeletal Sketch (for long passages). Then, use your Headline List or Skeletal Sketch to assist you in answering all the questions that accompany the passage.

4. Before answering each question, identify it as either a General question or a Specific question. Use the 7 strategies for Reading Comprehension to assist you in answering the questions.

5. On the GMAT, you will typically see three questions on short passages and four questions on long passages. However, in *The Official Guides*, the number of questions that you will see for each particular passage will vary significantly. As such, use the following modified timing guidelines during your practice:

For short passages: Spend approximately two to three minutes reading and creating your Headline List. Spend approximately 60 seconds answering General questions and between 60 to 90 seconds answering Specific questions.

For long passages: Spend approximately three to four minutes reading and creating your Skeletal Sketch. Spend approximately 60 seconds answering General questions and between 60 to 90 seconds answering Specific questions.

In general, simply use the following timing formula for each passage:

(# of Questions) × 2 = Total # of Minutes You Should Spend

This total number of minutes includes time for reading the passage, creating a Headline List or Skeletal Sketch, and answering all the questions.

mba**Mission**

Every candidate has a unique story to tell.

We have the creative experience to help you tell yours.

We are **mbaMission**, published authors with elite MBA experience who will work with you one-on-one to craft complete applications that will force the admissions committees to take notice. Benefit from straightforward guidance and personal mentorship as you define your unique attributes and reveal them to the admissions committees via a story only you can tell.

We will guide you through our "Complete Start to Finish Process":

- ☑ Candidate assessment, application strategy and program selection
- ☑ Brainstorming and selection of essay topics
- ☑ Outlining and essay structuring
- ☑ Unlimited essay editing
- ☑ Letter of recommendation advice
- ☑ Resume construction and review
- ☑ Interview preparation, mock interviews and feedback
- ☑ Post-acceptance and scholarship counseling

Monday Morning Essay Tip: Overrepresenting Your Overrepresentation

Many in the MBA application pool—particularly male investment bankers—worry that they are overrepresented. While you cannot change your work history, you can change the way you introduce yourself to admissions committees. Consider the following examples:

Example 1: "As an investment banking analyst at Bank of America, I am responsible for creating Excel models...."
Example 2: "At 5:30 pm, I could rest easy. The deadline for all other offers had passed. At that point, I knew...."

In the first example, the candidate starts off by mistakenly introducing the reader to the very over-representation that he/she should be trying to avoid emphasizing. In the second example, the banker immerses the reader in an unraveling mystery. This keeps the reader intrigued and focused on the applicant's story and actions rather than making the specific job title and responsibilities the center of the text. While each applicant's personal situation is different, every candidate can approach his/her story so as to mitigate the effects of overrepresentation.

To schedule a free consultation and read more than fifty Monday Morning Essay Tips, please visit our website:
www.mbamission.com